Welcome to the third edition of SCENES, an issue dedicated mostly to world film, in particular French and Italian. There is a large retrospective article on Catherine Deneuve, charting her long and varied life on screen, from her early days with Luis Bunuel and Jacques Demy, all the way to her most recent pictures. It's a remarkable run to say the least. There is a chat with Peter Riva, Marlene Dietrich's grandson, who talks about the German icon's career and his memories of her, and a piece on French director Bertrand Blier, including articles on his key films and a Q and A. I have also included a large article on the late French actor Michel Piccoli, and a piece about Antonioni's "Trilogy of Discontent". A varied set indeed...

- Editor, Chris Wade.

CONTENTS

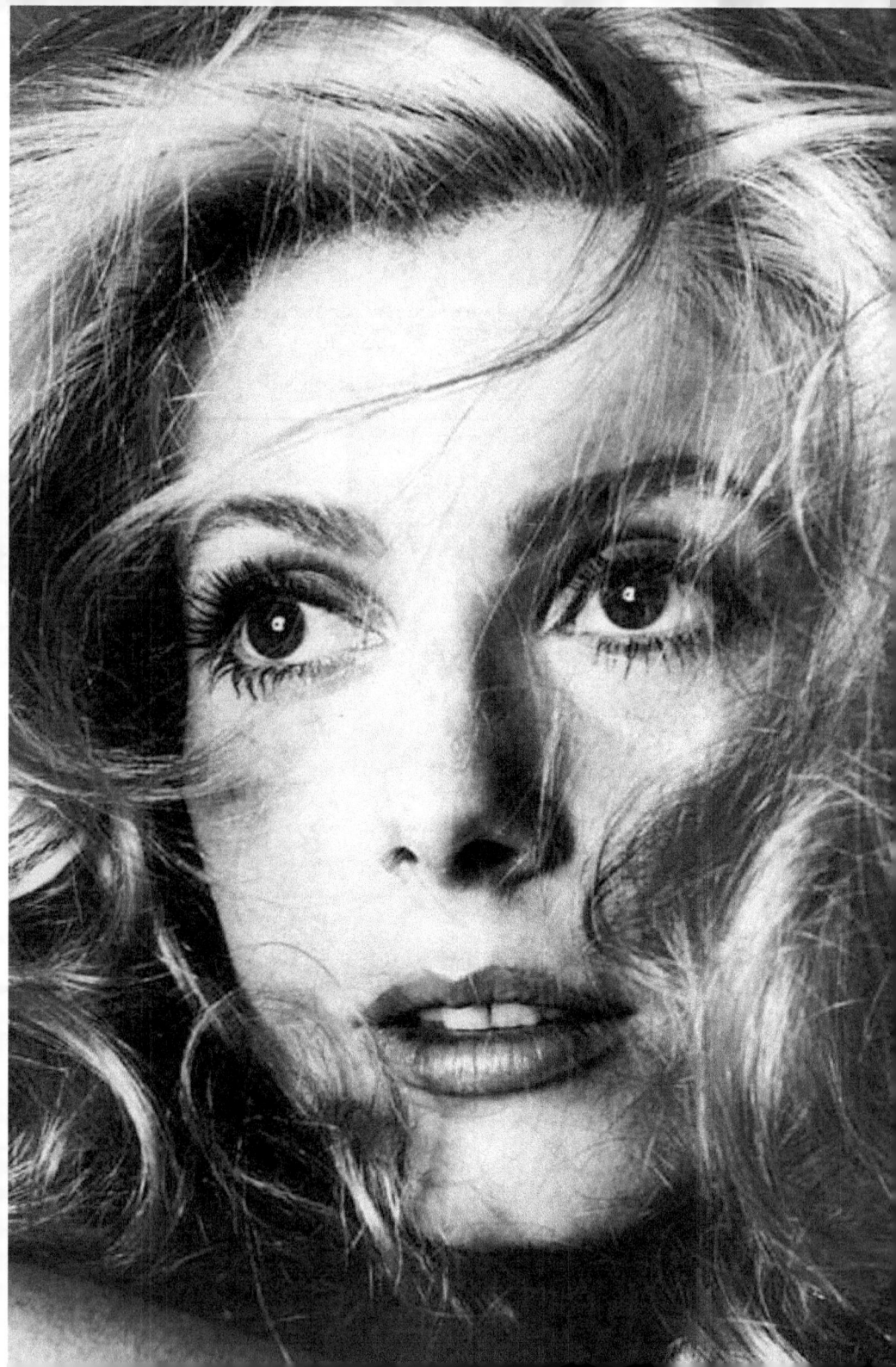

CATHERINE DENEUVE

She's been the queen of French cinema for over fifty years, has starred in some of the greatest films of all time, and even into her seventies she is still working as much as ever and getting the kind of roles that are the envy of other actresses. From her beginnings in the mid sixties with such films as The Umbrellas of Cherbourg, Repulsion, The Young Girls of Rochefort, Belle De Jour and Tristana, through seminal classics like The Last Metro, The Hunger, Indochine and more recent gems such as 8 Women, A Christmas Tale and The Truth, the name of Catherine Deneuve has always meant a certain kind of quality, a guarantee that you know the film you are watching is going to be of a certain quality. Here, CHRIS WADE explores a career (though Deneuve herself hates the word) that began during the French New Wave, working with such legends as Francois Truffaut, Luis Bunuel and Jacques Demy, and continues on to this day.

There are several well worn clichés that have followed Catherine Deneuve for over half a century now; the fact she's an ice queen; that she actually *is* the woman she played in Luis Bunuel's 1967 dark erotic masterpiece Belle De Jour; that she encapsulates everything there is to know about French sophistication; that she is the epitome of beauty; that she loved famous men such as Marcello Mastroianni, Francois Truffaut and David Bailey. Some of these things are true of course, but others are misconceptions and exaggerations which tire Deneuve herself. For me, Catherine Deneuve does represent a certain kind of European beauty, but for the most part I view her as a true artist, one of the world's greatest actresses who though an icon of glamour and beauty, has never let fame take over her life, and has hung tightly on to her credibility despite fifty years of prying and speculation. For me, Deneuve brings to mind countless wonderful films, numerous masterpieces, and the guarantee that she is going to impress in every given film. Going through her filmography hammers home the theory that she is one of the finest screen actors in history.

Catherine Fabienne Dorleac was born in Paris in 1943, the daughter of two French stage actors, Francoise Dorleac and Maurice Dorleac. Though she had no ambitions to act herself, she followed in her parents' and older sister Francoise's foot steps and began to land parts in films. Her screen debut came in 1957's Les Collegiennes, she casually acted more and was then cast in Roger Vadim's L'Homme a femmes in 1960. This was an important period of blossoming for Deneuve, who grew confident as an actor and married Vadim in 1961. The pair divorced however around the time she was cast as the lead in Jacques Demy's musical The Umbrellas of Cherbourg. The movie made her a star and established her as one of French cinema's leading lights.

From here on she worked solidly, often appearing in five or more films

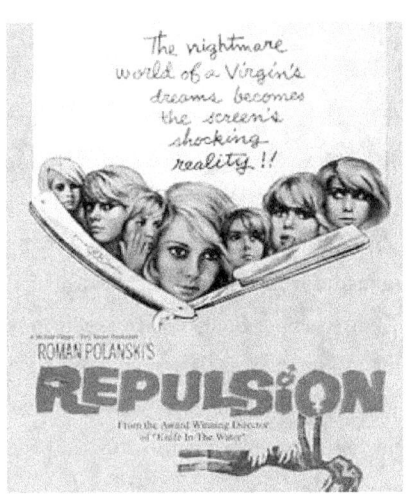

a year. The first big success after her work with Demy was Repulsion (1965). The film came at a vital time for director Roman Polanski, when he decided to move to London rather than return to Paris or indeed his family's original homeland, Poland. Settling in England's capital, he set about making his first film there. "Repulsion," he later said, "was my discovery of London. I was suddenly overwhelmed by the Anglo Saxon world... and I was tremendously inspired." Polanski came up with the idea for Repulsion with Gerard Brach, and a script was put together in Paris. They opted for something more

commercial than originally intended, and set about putting together a psychological horror film from the perspective of a woman. The tiny budget of 65,000 was raised by the Compton Pictures Company and filming began.

Polanski, though shooting in England, decided to cast a French actress, Catherine Deneuve, who was already well known for her work with Demy. One may have thought that Polanksi had enough on his plate, shooting in a place he knew very little, populated by people speaking a language he barely understood, but adding a French lead proved an inspired choice. Deneuve plays an inward, isolated young woman, alienated from all around her; in fact, her Frenchness only widens the gap between her and the Londoners around her, whether they be buskers, customers at the hair stylists where she works, or potential male suitors after her heart. At first, we see Deneuve's disconnected state as depression, something which may be solved with rest. However, it soon becomes apparent that the main thing which drives her mental torment is the repulsion she feels when a male comes near her, or makes a sexual advance. She begins to have hallucinations, hears things and sees terrible sights. The film turns darkly sinister when she ends up killing a young man who has been trying to get her to go on a date and places his corpse in the bath. From here on, isolated in the flat she shares with her sister (but who has gone away on holiday with her married lover), Deneuve's Carol suffers a total meltdown which becomes more horrific and harrowing for the viewer (and Carol too) as the film storms towards its chilling climax.

Polanski directs the film with claustrophobic intimacy, making us not mere observers of Carol's breakdown but active participants. Indeed, the viewer is aligned with Carol so we too become confused about what is real and what is a vision of madness. Though Deneuve is responsible for providing the film's core and heart, it would not have been so effective without Roman's confident guidance. We enter another world from the first frame to the end, and though it is far from a pleasant one, we are hundred percent invested in Carol's terrifying ordeal.

Critics have read Carol's reaction to the male in various ways; some have seen it as a guttural reaction against her sister's lover, who she despises and in some ways sets off the whole film; others believe Carol may have been abused as a child; while some have even said that Carol is a kind of warped feminist icon in that she rebels against what is expected of a woman, to be taken out by men with a hope that she will eventually sleep with them. She finds intimacy repulsive, and whatever triggered this off, Carol is on a one way ticket to oblivion.

Deneuve delivers a truly electrifying performance in a film which rightfully brought her world wide attention and helped her become a major star. She embodies Carol, the ice cold outsider, the

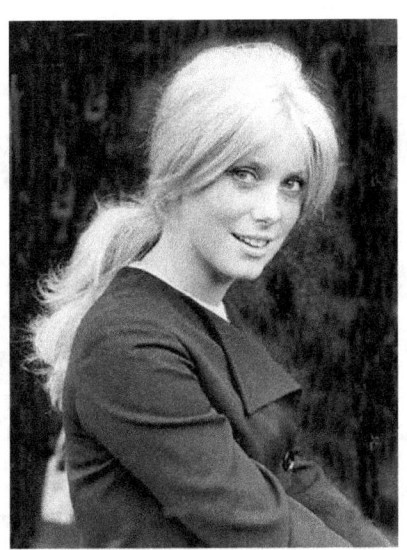

isolated female lost in a man's world, to a tee. This is where her image as cinema's ice queen began, solidified of course by her role three years later in Bunuel's Belle De Jour. She is at the start of a marvellous career here, delivering a performance which is much more mature and assured than might seem possible.

The film was a hit upon release, won major prizes at the Berlin International Film Festival and garnered enthusiasm from the critics. The New York Times raved it was "An absolute knockout of a movie in the psychological horror line has been accomplished by Roman Polanski in his first English-language film." Not only is Repulsion now rightly seen as a landmark film of the 1960s, it is also recognised as a trailblazer for indie cinema, horror in particular, and hundreds if not thousands of films have borrowed its sense of isolation, doom and depiction of mental torment. The idea of a young woman in an apartment which begins to come alive in its very walls to consume her is a scenario that has been repeated and aped time and time again in the horror genre, though Polanski's interest in the psychological lifts it from being a mere thrill-fest and into something much more multi layered. Deneuve's performance, too, is vital in its success.

Deneuve has continually stated that the shoot, despite its dark subject matter, was a fun and fulfilling one. Speaking to Film Comment, Deneuve said "It's funny because three of us were French: Roman, who, despite being Polish, spoke French all

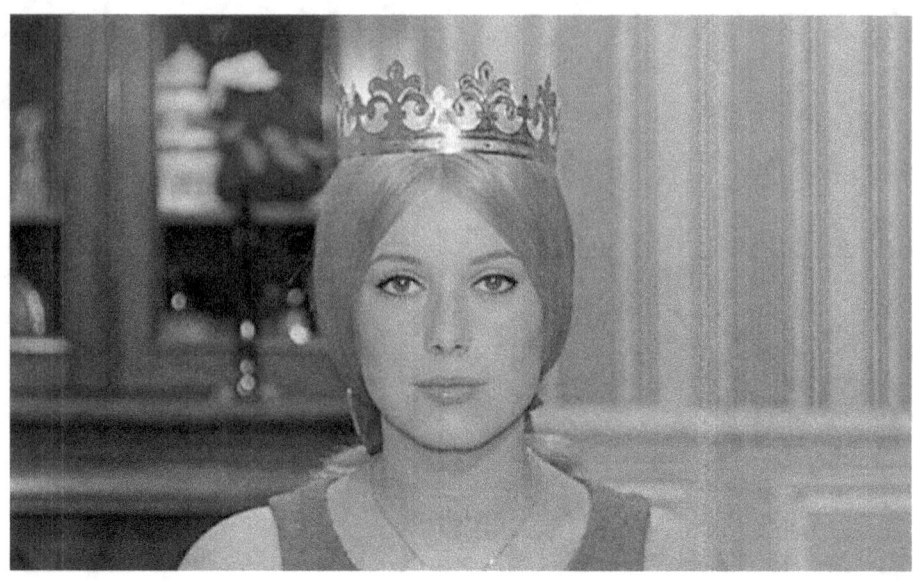

the time, Gérard Brach, and me. We really were the Three Musketeers. Everybody else on set was British. Roman knew exactly how to be respected by the crew, he was no pushover. But because we spoke French, we experienced the making of that film a little from the sidelines, in a rather unique atmosphere. We were a core within the team. I felt very, very close to Roman. That's the film I feel I helped make. The producers were used to producing porn. It was a small budget film and for them, nothing of great consequence... The experience with Roman was very important to me."

She continued to work after the film's success. Released the same year she became the glacial queen of desire in Belle de Jour, Deneuve starred alongside her sister Francoise Dorleac in The Young Girls of Rochefort (1967), Catherine's second collaboration with the legendary writer/director Jacques Demy. Like their earlier film together, The Umbrellas of Cherbourg, The Young Girls of Rochefort is a sweet, colourful and hugely enjoyable light musical drama, though in some ways it may just be a stronger film. It does too, sadly, have a somewhat bittersweet feel to it, given that poor Francoise died the year it was released, aged only 25, in a car accident. Catherine was of course devastated, and in due course the film would become their most memorable dual offering to the world. It was a huge hit, if not a sensation when it was released, not just in France but the world over, and today is still a classic of the musical genre.

Francoise and Catherine play two sisters (as so memorably explained in one of the film's most best songs) getting on with their lives; Deneuve gives music lessons, Francoise teaches ballet. They both dream of a bigger world outside Rochefort, and they are promised such a thing when they begin to court two young men from the travelling fair who have arrived in the seaside town. Among the rest of the cast are Danielle Darrieux as their mother Yvonne, West Side Story legend George Chakiris as one of the carnies, and the wonderful Michel Piccoli as Yvonne's old fiancée. There is also a notable effort from the legendary Gene Kelly, the man who defined the Hollywood musical, in his first film for over a decade.

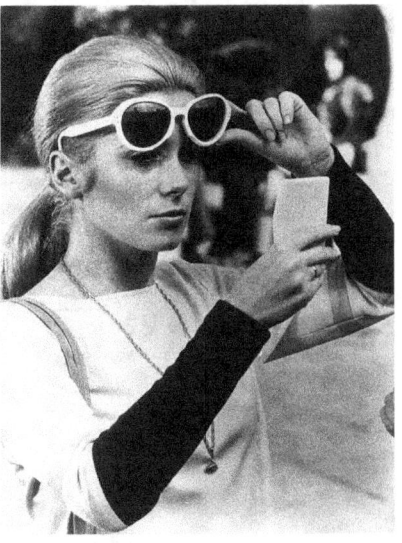

The Young Girls of Rochefort is an endlessly charming film, with plenty of good songs, bright costumes, lively performances and a general mood of care free jollity, even when melancholic or lightly mournful. It is of course, also extremely of its time,

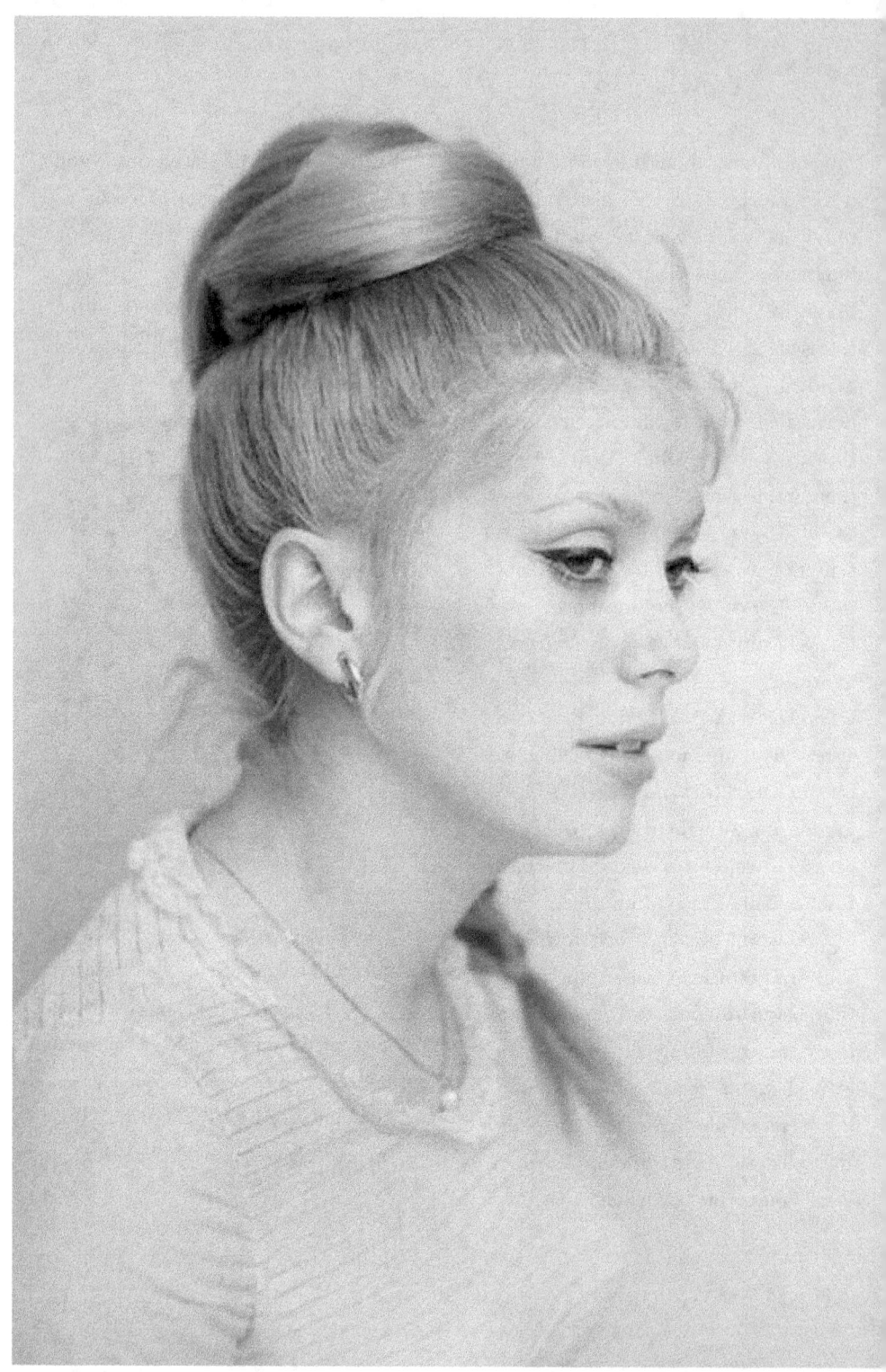

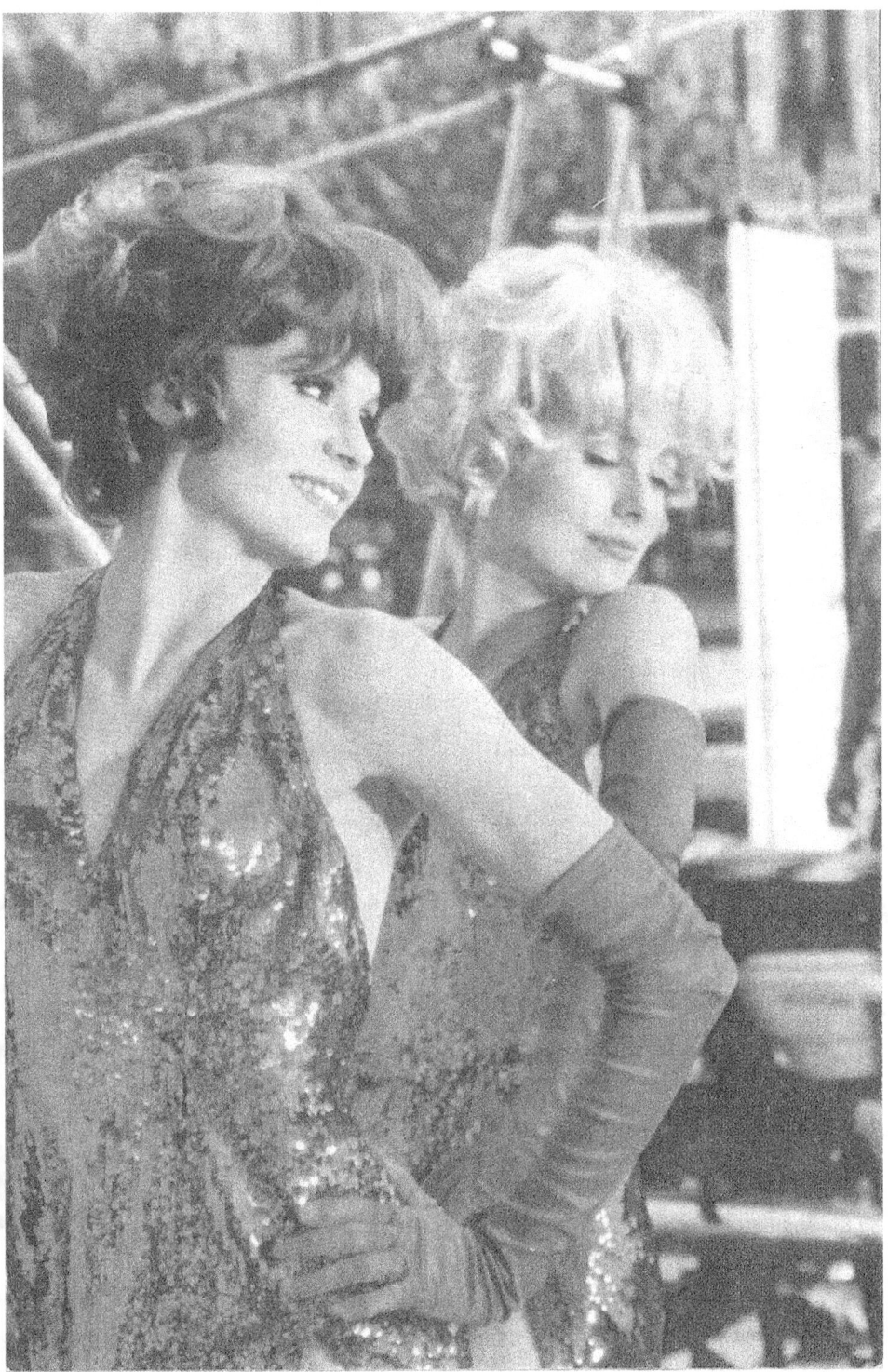

with the music and visuals so quintessentially sixties that one cannot help but think of Austin Powers, but thankfully infrequently. Fans of French cinema, of course, will love it, and delight in the accents which are often rapidly reciting the lyrics at an alarming rate, and the typically French quirks. If not for the French accents however, the film could easily - on a visual level - pass for an old Hollywood musical, with Demy totally nailing the look and vibe of that beloved era.

This is a film which not only highlights the very unique and sizeable talent of Demy, but the early magic of Catherine Deneuve who, though dubbed in song, radiates throughout. While I believe much of Deneuve's strongest work has come in the decades which followed this era, she is brilliant here and vitally fresh, at the very early stages of a marvellous career; as is Francoise, who would have surely gone on to more greatness had her life not been cut so tragically short.

This homage to the golden era of Hollywood musicals is one of the finest entries in the genre of the era, a masterfully crafted visual and auditory delight which more than deserves its reputation as a seminal picture. Its influence remains as alive as ever, as evident in the smash hit musical La La Land, which one might say did much more than lift a bit of inspiration from The Young Girls of Rochefort.

An essential version of the film is the BFI's two DVD release, overseen by Demy's widow, Agnes Verda, which also features an interview with Deneuve about the making of the film and a 25th anniversary documentary shot by Verda, which features Deneuve heading back to Rochefort.

But Belle De Jour is the film which most people associate with Catherine Deneuve, despite the fact her film appearances are now in the triple figures. Deneuve has often spoken of how journalists seem to associate her with the cold and distant woman of Luis Bunuel's 1967 masterpiece; and the fact that this character becomes a call girl in an attempt to "feel" something more than the strange numbness she does must make this association somewhat troubling.

She plays Severine, a young housewife with a comfortable life in her marriage to Dr Pierre Serizy. Though in love, they do not have a sex life and she is incapable of letting herself go in the bedroom. We are shown their world, her frigidity and negative attitude towards her husband's friend, Henri (played by the brilliant Michel Piccoli), who gives her a look which makes her uncomfortable and feel objectified. When she learns of a high class brothel, she becomes curious. As her erotic day dreams become more intense (in one she is pelted with shit by her husband and Henri, in the other raped and whipped by two coachmen) she decides to head down to the brothel, where she meets the Madame, Anais (Genevieve Page). At first she is shy and reluctant for the clients to touch her, but soon eases into her role as a lady of the night.

Soon though, things get out of hand when she becomes involved with a gangster called Marcel, a man who brings the same sensations she feels in her fantasies into the real world.

It's well known that Luis Bunuel did not want Catherine Deneuve for the role, and was perhaps a little distant with her during filming due to this fact. He even told associates that she didn't get the role and had no idea how to play it. Later of course he changed his mind, for it is undoubtable that Catherine is nothing short of brilliant in her part. She did not enjoy the experience one bit, finding Luis distant and cold. In their first meeting over dinner the only bit of advice he gave her was "Don't do anything. And above all, don't perform." Deneuve certainly took this on board, but left with the knowledge that Bunuel really did not like actors. She also had issues with the nudity. "I felt they showed more of me than they'd said they were going to," she said in 2004. "There

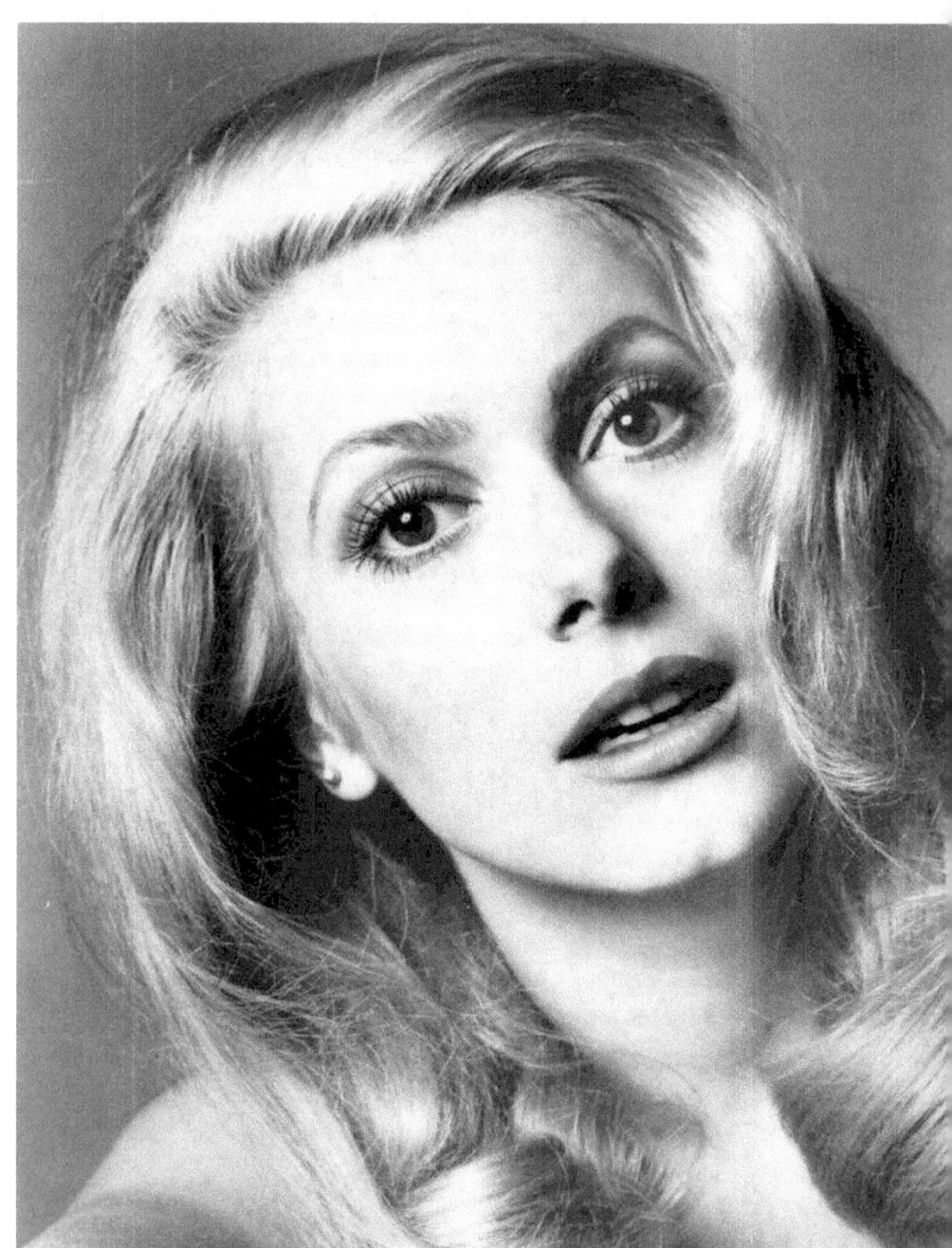

14

were moments when I felt totally used. I was very unhappy."

Embellishing further, she told the Guardian: "Well, I think it was difficult for him, coping with his deafness. Some people said he was not that deaf, but I think, when you don't hear very well and when you're tired, everything sinks into a buzz, and it is very hard. French is not his language, so on Belle de Jour, I'm sure that it was much more of an effort for him to have to explain. I've always thought that he likes actors, up to a point. I think he likes very much the idea of the film, and to write it. But I had the impression that the film-making was not what he preferred to do. He had to go through actors, and he liked them if they were easy, simple, not too much fuss. He would say very little to actors. But then, there weren't many ways to do the scenes. You couldn't really fool around with the script - it was very precise."

Somehow, Deneuve got through the filming with no real issues and the film was greeted with an almost ecstatic reception, bagging awards and rave notices all across the world. The Los Angeles Times wrote "It is one of life's surprising ironies that the great Spanish director Luis Buñuel, having turned out a succession of masterpieces with no particular box office movie, should now be enjoying the first big commercial success of his career with a movie which is less than a masterpiece, but sexy. And in colour. Belle de Jour is more interesting and provocative than the great run of pictures one ever sees. Buñuel's handling of color is gorgeous. And the acting is impeccable. Miss Deneuve has a rare, cool elegance which suggests far more fire than it reveals."

Bunuel had been making films since the 1920s and though enjoying success with the likes of Un Chein Andalou, L'age Dor and Diary of a Chamber Maid, he had never enjoyed the kind of attention Belle De Jour received. The film set in motion the remarkable last decade of his career, where he went from masterpiece to masterpiece. Belle De Jour though, thanks largely to Deneuve's terrific effort, remains his most famous and iconic work.

Writing about the film over thirty years since its release, Roger Ebert still thought it a classic. "It is possibly the best-known erotic film of modern times, perhaps the best," he stated. "That's because it understands eroticism from the inside-out-- understands how it exists not in sweat and skin, but in the imagination. The film is elegantly mounted -- costumes, settings, decor, hair, clothes--and languorous in its pacing. Severine's fate seems predestined. So does that of her husband, who as a weak man is swept away by the implacable strength of his wife's desire. The best stylistic touches are the little ones, which someone unfamiliar with Bunuel might miss (although they work even if you don't notice them). The subtle use of meows on the soundtrack; what do they represent? Only Severine knows. The weary wisdom about human nature: After Severine refuses an early client, Anais sends in another girl, then takes Severine into the next room to watch through a peephole and learn. "That is disgusting," Severine says, turning away. Then she turns back and looks through the peephole again.

The fact it has become Deneuve's signature role is somewhat ironic, given the unpleasantness of the shoot itself. Yet she is perfect as the distracted female, often transfixed by her fantasies and out of tune with the world around her. As in Repulsion, she cannot bring herself to be freed into sexuality; unlike Repulsion however, she does not descend into madness and finds a way to bring the fantasies to vivid life. But Repulsion and Belle De Jour are both ambiguous about the roots of Deneuve's cold stares and frigidity, which of course makes both characters in each film all the more appealing and mysterious. In many ways she is Belle De Jour, not just the character but the movie itself; and as much as it is characteristic of Bunuel and so very clearly his work, it feels just as much to be Deneuve's creation. It may not be Catherine's personal favourite of her movies (nor mine for that matter) but it's one she will forever be associated with.

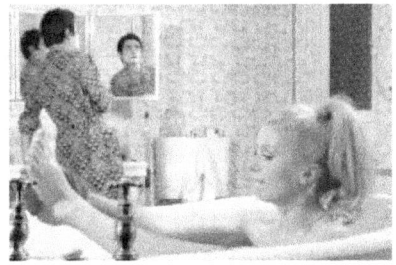

Manon 70 (1968) was another cold Deneuve performance, this time as a glacial model being used by her brother to drain finances from an older, wealthy admirer, all the while battling with her new lover. Manon 70's only flaw is that the characters are hard to care about, but Deneuve is as striking and appealing as ever.

Next up for Deneuve was a lead role in Alain Cavalier's romantic drama, La Chamade (1968), based on the book by Francoise Sagan. She plays Lucile, a seemingly care free young woman who is the mistress of the wealthy businessman Charles, played by Michel Piccoli. Though she has a good time with Charles, and he in turn treats her well, he is perhaps a little too old for her. Suddenly she meets a man her own age, Antoine (Roger Van Hool), while out for the evening. As Charles can clearly see, she is instantly attracted to the younger man. As expected she falls in love with Antoine, who gets her a job at a publishing firm, though she proves incapable of holding it down. Things become much more serious when she falls pregnant to her new man. But will she keep the baby, and will Lucile come to her senses and see that Charles is the man for her?

Coming right after the smash success of Belle De Jour, it's no surprise that La Chamade did well commercially. It was also warmly received in the press. The New York Times wrote of it: "Alain Cavalier's French screen adaptation of Francoise Sagan's 1966 novel, is like a glass paperweight in which something small and exotic has been embedded—a seahorse, perhaps. It is elegant and lucid, something very pleasant to have around even though it's not exactly an objet d'art of the first order." They also commented on how plastic Deneuve had looked in the recent The April Fools (explained by the fact she did not enjoy the shoot one bit), and added that she is "very much alive as the unhappy Lucile. Miss Deneuve suffers—always beautifully—the guilts and betrayals and compromises that dilute the value of love, which, in Sagan's world, is both the literal and figurative currency.

Deneuve, in my eyes, is excellent in the film and she proved here that she was not just the ice queen of Repulsion and Belle De Jour. In La Chamade she desperately wants love, craves affection, and she gets herself in a spot of trouble trying to find the right man to get it from. Though not cold, she does have an air of melancholia about her, which adds a quiet sadness to her predicament amidst the love triangle, and the fact she is beautifully costumed throughout by Yves Saint Laurent only makes it more poignant, the crisp and superficial surface masking

an inner conflict. Cavalier, certainly a lesser figure of the French New Wave, had by the late sixties gone into making more straight forward and commercial pictures than some of his contemporaries; and while La Chamade is certainly conventional, bordering on melodramatic at times, it is engaging and though provoking with its solid acting and ironic twists. Piccoli is watchable as ever, here playing a man who knows it pays to be patient, but like a father he waits with rolling eyes for his mistress to return to the good life he can provide her. Still, this is a film quietly dominated by the presence of a Deneuve whose every movement and word we hang upon.

In retrospect, 1969's The April Fools does indeed look like an odd choice of film for Catherine Deneuve, a woman so closely associated with French cinema and not someone to make an international film choice too lightly. When you consider its time of release, Deneuve had already worked with the likes of Jacques Demy, Luis Bunuel and Roman

Polanski, and the very same year she was to act for Francois Truffaut, the leading figure of the French New Wave. The April Fools then, seems an even stranger choice when aligned with her other work of the period. But though this typical Hollywood romance is often clichéd, it has a lot going for it and is actually much more enjoyable and effective than you first might believe.

It stars the brilliant Jack Lemmon as Howard Brubaker, a man trapped in a loveless marriage who is promoted by his boss, Ted Gunther (Peter Lawford). Howard attends a party hosted by Ted and finds himself befuddled by the swinging activities, the shallowness of the guests and the superficial air. One person he does warm to however (and understandably so) is Ted's wife, Catherine, played by Catherine Deneuve. Ted, a womaniser himself, has insisted Howard try it on with a woman and taking up the challenge he accidentally chats up Ted's wife. Increasingly frustrated by her marriage, Catherine accepts and leaves with Howard. The pair quickly fall in love and speedily plan on abandoning their loveless marriages.

The April Fools could not have been a more out of date picture if it tried, a conventional romantic comedy set against a swinging sixties/Austin Powers style backdrop. While the trendy films of the time, such as The Graduate and Easy Rider, celebrated the outsider, The April Fools was full of characters embracing the more phony sides of the loose and free era but contradicting themselves with their wealth and shallowness. This said, The April Fools is poking fun at the fashionable people who hypocritically groove to the hippy music in their expensive clothes and flash apartments. Howard and Catherine are outsiders, two people who do not fit in with the world they have found themselves in. Catherine is much deeper than the other airheads Ted surrounds himself with, while the sensitive and rather clumsy Howard could not be more different than his boss. They naturally slip

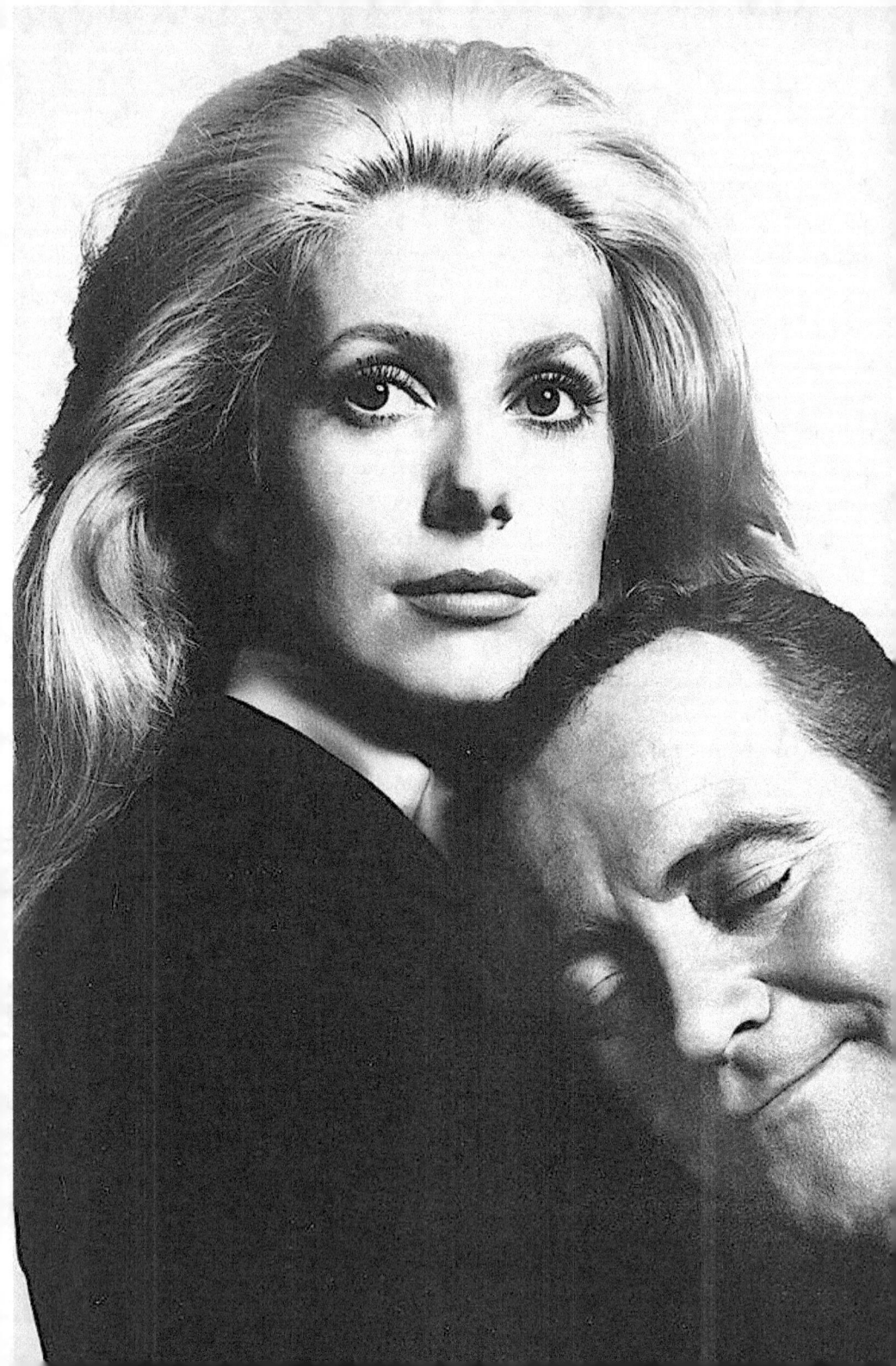

away together out of the fakeness of the big city and long for a purer, more honest life.

The script itself is not so sharp and it is littered with clichés, but the film is rescued by its performances. Lemmon is wonderful and works wonders with what he is given, while Deneuve (herself a quick replacement for Shirley MacLaine who was lined up for the role but was too busy to take the movie on) has never been as cool, calm and collected. She is quietly effective in a role that requires the distant air she is famous for, a woman who is indifferent to Ted's meaningless, capitalist high life and equally unimpressed by it. Dressed as she is by Yves Saint Laurent, she also looks stunning. Credit must also go to the "spouses"; Lawford is brilliant as the philandering Ted, while Sally Kellerman is heartlessly hilarious as Howard's wife.

The film performed well at the box office but attracted mixed reviews. It's certainly not one of the finest films of Deneuve's long and varied career, but is definitely a pleasant viewing experience.

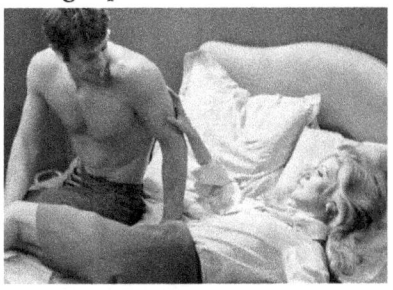

Mississippi Mermaid (1969) was her first collaboration with Francois Truffaut, who she would work with again on The Last Metro in 1980. Jean Paul Belmondo plays Louis, a rich owner of a tobacco plantation near the Indian Ocean. He begins a correspondence with a young woman who he then becomes engaged to. When she turns up on the island where he lives, she is not the same girl he saw in the photos. Despite this fact though, he decides to marry her anyway. (To be fair, if Catherine Deneuve turned up you'd go ahead and marry her too!)

One of Truffaut's more straight forward films, it is deceptively complex, and he directs with a sense of control and understanding of the thriller genre. Deneuve is fabulous too as the woman who is not what she seems; not quite the ice queen of Bunuel's world, but just as enigmatic and darkly appealing.

It's funny to think that of the two films Deneuve and Bunuel made together, Belle De Jour is the one which has become the most remembered and iconic, while in my view, Tristana (1970) is the much more poignant and engaging film; and dare I say it, the one which has aged the best. In Belle De Jour, Deneuve was the perfect ice cold woman of frigidity, the kind of woman who remains a mystery to a man, closed up and locked within herself but attempting to be freed. In Tristana, she plays a much more multi layered role, that of a young woman in 1920s small town Spain who, upon the death of her mother, is taken on by an ageing nobleman called Don Lope, played by the brilliant Fernando Rey. Though hard-up himself, he retains an air of dignity as all upper class men do even when the money isn't coming in.

But Don Lope is all about surface; if he dresses and acts the part, can hire a maid and have enough to live and get by (though at one point he confesses he is down to his last egg and offers it to Tristana over himself), he will remain noble. His downfall begins when he urges Tristana to not only be his adopted daughter but also his lover. She agrees, reluctantly, and eventually begins to resent the old man. Had he simply offered to care for her, she would have carried on respecting him. However, with his passion he degrades himself and sours the bond they might have had. She begins to see a young artist on the side and when an illness strikes her unexpectedly, she must return to the care of Don Lope. Living as an amputee, she finds herself forced to marry the old man. But what will become of this strange marriage, and Don Lope himself?

Tristana is a brilliant film, carefully paced and with wonderfully written characters which are believable in all their flaws and shortcomings. Bunuel is not embittered by humanity, only honest with what it can reduce itself to. He directs with his usual assured confidence, gracefully gliding as an observer and never making the camera apparent. Indeed, this is the camera as a human eye, not a tool of trickery and technique.

The film features two very fine performances from Deneuve and Rey; Rey goes from being the harsh but seemingly decent man, ready to take on the young woman, to the rather pathetic, ailing sham, a man living a lie with a woman who has grown to hate him. Catherine Deneuve puts in one of the finest efforts of her whole career (though she would never class her film work as a career), beginning the film as a sweet girl with a child-like sense of wonderment, but ending it as a one legged bitter woman who resents the man who has promised to care for her yet does not have the means to do so. It's a complex performance, but Deneuve makes it look simple; this is the journey of a woman, treated as a plaything, a commodity, yearning for freedom and then having her leg taken from her in the cruellest of dark ironies, though it is in the amputation that her new life truly begins. Don Lope's demise and Tristana's cold and cruel treatment of him towards the end of the picture is an act of revenge for his incestuous violation and the destruction of her innocence.

The roots of Tristana began in 1962 when Bunuel and Julio Alejandro wrote the screenplay. But the script was rejected by the Ministry of Culture, deemed offensive, so Bunuel worked on other films instead. When Bunuel returned to his birth country of Spain in December of 1968 he was approached about finally doing Tristana. Though he initially wanted to make a film called The Monk, eventually he was persuaded to approach the Tristana script once backing was obtained. Bunuel had not wanted Deneuve for Belle De Jour as we all know, and once again for Tristana he was convinced by the distributors that Deneuve would be a good commercial choice. Having not enjoyed her experience of making Belle De Jour, Deneuve found Bunuel easier on Tristana and preferred the shooting of it, as recounted in her published film diaries. Still, she often found Bunuel difficult and cut off, but at least she understood him more and his approach to making a film.

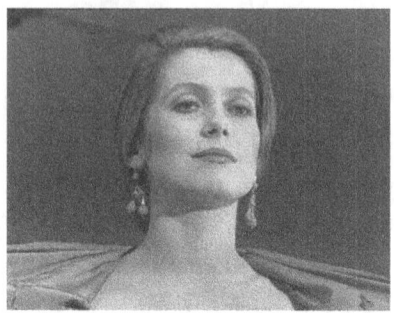

"He had a great sense of humour," Deneuve said in one interview. "But we got along much better on Tristana than on Belle de Jour. On Belle de Jour, the producer was very protective and we were very separated and it was very hard for me. Frankly, he was quite different and I think I know why. It was the first time he had been able to go back to Spain since Viridiana; it was a book that he had always wanted to do so he was very happy to go back to Spain to do it. He was a lot more open. We even had dinner together in my house, which was something very exceptional. I could feel he was very different, and being surrounded by the Spanish language was much easier for him. Everything went very smoothly and well. Tristana is one of my favourite films."

Bunuel saw Don Lope as an embodiment of his father, and with his handling of the old man he clearly sympathised with him. Speaking to the New York Times after its release, Bunuel said "Personally, I'm monogamous and discreet. An old man can easily make a fool of himself. Like Don Lope in Tristana, I believe in a chaste eroticism. You can attribute that to my Jesuit education. Sexual pleasure for me is directly linked with the idea of sin and only exists in a religious context. The sexual act cannot be reduced to a chapter on hygienics; it is an exciting, dark, sinful, diabolical experience. Sex is a black tarantula and sex without religion is like an egg without salt. In the Summa Theologica, Saint Thomas says that fornication between man and woman, even if they be married, is nevertheless a venial sin. Now, I think that's a very sexy idea! Sin multiplies the possibilities of desire."

Tristana, while not a sensation on the scale of their previous film together, was a success. It received the Academy Award nomination for Best Foreign Language Film, and has gone down as classic Bunuel. In my view, it may just be his finest film. It won the admiration of Alfred Hitchcock too, who sent Bunuel a note highlighting his jealousy of what he saw as some of Luis's more masterful shots. High praise indeed.

She was back with director Jacques Demy once again on Donkey Skin (1971), adapted from Charles Perrault's fairytale about the king who wants to marry his daughter. The princess, who dons a donkey skin the king gifted her and flees his unwanted advances, is played beautifully by Deneuve, always at her best under the direction of the understanding Demy.

It Only Happens to Others (1971), written and directed by Nadine Trintignant, was the first film real life couple Marcello Mastroianni and Catherine Deneuve made together. This tragic French drama has the iconic duo as a couple who struggle through life after losing their baby. The film stings more because Nadine herself went through this ordeal in real life. It's a serious issue and dealt with in an adult way. The two leads play it with respectful dignity, never resorting to clichéd schmaltz of the kind you might see in Hollywood mush. It was a big hit in France, but is sadly buried in the vaults of time. It Only Happens to Others, available on DVD if you look hard enough, is definitely deserving of a reappraisal.

In the crime thriller Un Flic (1972), she was with Alain Delon as the mistress of Richard Crenna. She provided the slick beauty but also the film's most complex character. Again, she proved she was never in a film as dressing alone. She manages to give Cathy much more depth and mystery than the average actress in such a film might have.

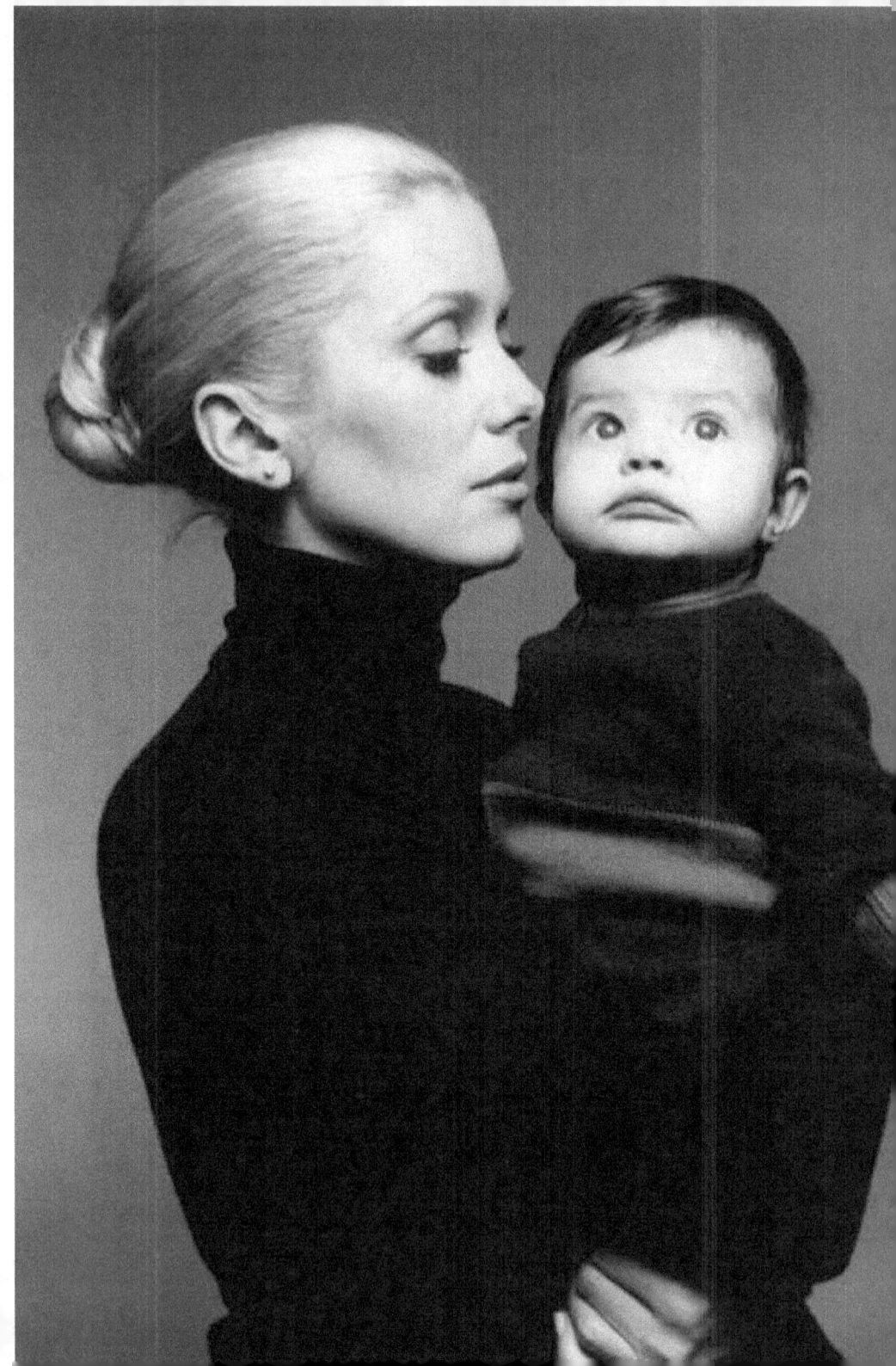

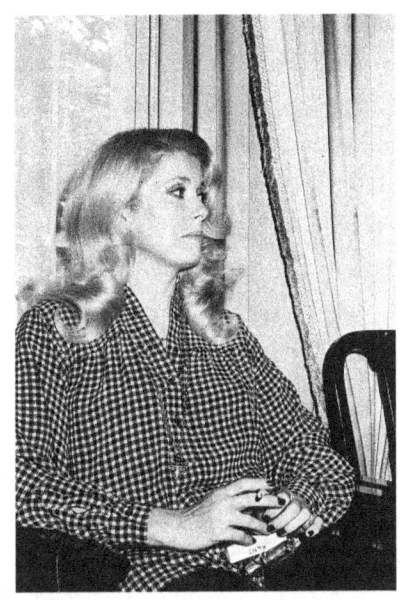

The third film Mastroianni and Deneuve made together was in many ways their best, the lightly comic, A Slightly Pregnant Man (1973). Twenty years before the release of the shockingly bad Arnold Schwarzenegger vehicle Junior, often seen as the first pregnant-man comedy, Marcello Mastroianni was the expectant male in Jacques Demy's silly but engaging French exploration into gender roles and expectations, exploring these issues without degenerating into farce. He plays Marco, a driving instructor who one day begins to feel bloated, blaming it on the housekeeper's chicken recipe. However, when visiting the doctor he is told that he is in fact carrying a child, perhaps because the hormones in the chicken, of which he been eating too much, has boosted his femininity and made him pregnant. Everyone is scratching their heads, but the common theory is that he is a miracle of science. He becomes a celebrity, appears on chat shows and finds himself at the centre of a media circus. After this, other men around the world become pregnant. Or do they?

A Slightly Pregnant Man is the easier Deneuve/Mastroianni film to track down these days, it being available on a widely distributed DVD. It really is genuinely funny, with a sharp script, and is also wonderfully acted, especially by Marcello who is suitably dry throughout, raising genuine laughs when he's starting to notice the belly and stops dead in his tracks at the sight of a pregnant woman. In the first part of the film he nails the hardworking dad, tired out and a little peeved, always aware that he is trying to keep his head above water. When "pregnant", things change and his whole outlook alters. His work becomes a struggle but he is genuinely looking forward to the new arrival. He plays it brilliantly, and his chemistry with Deneuve is an added bonus, who is also charming in her role as the loving, doting wife. Alongside the two stars is the young Benjamin Legrand as their 8 year old son, also impressive in his part. It's just one of those films which runs smoothly, flies by in what feels like an instant and rarely puts a foot wrong.

The film did quite well upon release, though it did not set the world alight. Reviewing it at the time, Jonathan Rosenbaum wrote that "A Slightly Pregnant Man doesn't really work, but it is a weird kind of fun." Few critics have taken it serious down the years, but perhaps they have missed the point. Time Out wrote "Demy's usually feather light touch deserts him with this clodhopping farce", while Slant, retrospectively reviewing the DVD release, called it "a provocative, if minor, Demy film." Yet I feel of all the comedies Marcello and Deneuve have made through the years, this is one of the best because it raises issues while telling its story. This is a film about equality, fairness and gender definition. In the feminist world, a man carrying a baby feels like the perfect step forward, sharing the hardships of women everywhere.

There is also another way to read the film. Demy was gay and married to Agnes Varda, though he revealed little about their private life. So is this film a disguised longing for a child of his own, the need to carry and be close to his own kin, to wonder what it is like to bare that responsibility, that honour? Or is it a progressive call for role reversals, a new age of equality, where men and women take on responsibilities together?

Deneuve had already given some of her best performances on film for director Luis Bunuel, namely in Belle

De Jour and Tristana, so what is firstly interesting about this oddity, known in English as The Lady in Red Boots (1974), is the fact that she is directed by Luis's son, Juan Luis Bunuel. While the picture itself is now all but forgotten, it is a solid addition to the surrealist film genre and, dare I say it, worthy of Juan's father's work, the master Luis himself. Catherine Deneuve is the lady of the title, more often than not wearing the said red boots, and most of the time clad in a poncho, long scarf and woolly white jumper. Fernando Rey, an actor known for his work in such Bunuel films as Tristana, That Obscure Object of Desire and The Discreet Charm of the Bourgeois, puts in an unsettling effort as a millionaire named Perrot, who first begins to stalk Deneuve and eventually begins to control her life. This is a film of images to behold, a pleasure to view for its visuals alone. It has an atmosphere all of its own, like a continuation of Luis Bunuel but with a lighter and dare I say more playfully surreal air about it.

Juan punctuates his films with unforgettable scenes; like when Deneuve as a young girl witnesses the death of a maid falling from a balcony (brilliantly, Deneuve herself stands beside her childhood counterpart, mimicking her younger self's movements perfectly); and most memorably when Rey visits a sleeping Deneuve and without waking her, plants a rose on her and then takes a picture. Deneuve puts in a mysterious and appealing performance as the enigmatic lady, and carries the film elegantly alongside seasoned pro Fernando Rey, who was, it has to be said, brilliant in everything he was in.

La Femme Aux Bottes ouges won't make any best-of lists you might chance upon, but it's a very engaging and ultimately memorable film from a man trying to establish himself out of the formidable and overbearing shadow of his genius father. In my view, with this striking film, he emerges from Bunuel's intimidating legacy with an admirable feat that, had you not seen the name on the credits, one might mistake for a lost Luis Bunuel gem recently unearthed from the vaults.

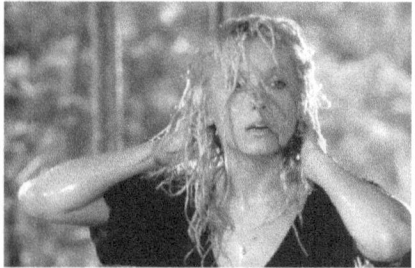

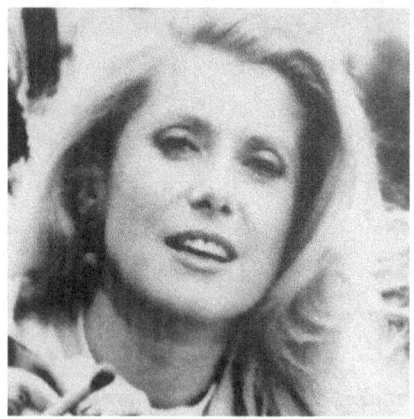

She made another trip to Hollywood for Hustle (1975) opposite Burt Reynolds. Though the film has dated a little today, it is still an intriguing crime story and was a massive hit upon release, making ten million dollars in a week alone. Robert Aldrich said he would only direct the film if they could get Deneuve to play the part of Nicole, the prostitute who Reynolds' police lieutenant falls for. Aldrich recalled: "We put up our money and went to Paris, and waited on the great lady for a week, and she agreed to do the picture."

Deneuve steals the film, dominating it with her effortlessly elegant performance. No one else could have made the call girl so graceful, and among the American actors she is by far the strongest performer.

While other European stars might have stuck around Hollywood longer, especially after such a success, Deneuve, not finding any of her offers appealing, went back to France. Firstly she played to her sexy image opposite Yves Montand in Lovers Like Us (1975). She portrays Nelly, a woman who has a change of heart and flees her wedding, and with the help of Montand gets a ticket to Paris. Montand goes back to his remote island life but finds that Nelly has followed him there, much to his irritation. When she damages his boat, it is clear that he will have to get used to life on the island with his new guest. The picture is good fun and Deneuve looks fabulous in it, but it could be said that, as Truffaut later observed, he felt Catherine should have been acting in weightier, more meaningful films. In 1979, Francois took action and came knocking on her door.

Though people popularly believe that Francois Truffaut's artistic peak was during the French New Wave boom of the late fifties and early sixties, with classic films like The 400 Blows and Jules and Jim, I argue that some of his best work was made during the wave's resurgence in the early 80s. Shortly before his untimely death in 1983, Truffaut made three extraordinary films, the first of these being 1980s The Last Metro, the second part in his proposed trilogy on the performing arts.

The film concerns a Parisian theatre still operating during Germany's occupation of France. The Montmatre was formally run by Lucas Steiner, a Jewish theatre director, who is now hiding underground in the basement as his wife, Marion Steiner (played by Catherine Deneuve), runs the establishment and stars as leading lady in their new production. Bernard Grainger (Gerard Depardieu), a womanising young actor, is cast as the lead, and Marion unexpectedly begins to develop feelings for him. As Lucas listens through the vents and writes down directorial ideas for later inspection, the anti-Semite theatre critic Daxiat begins to sniff around, and on top of organising the running of the troupe, Marion has to deal with unannounced visits from the Nazis who wish to examine the premises, including the basement, where her husband, who she is clearly falling out of love with, is kept secret. After Grainger beats up Daxiat in the street when he gives them a bad review (disgustingly highlighting inherent "Jewishness" in the play), it becomes clear he is part of the French Resistance. Will Bernard's fiery personality rouse suspicion and attract the attention of the Nazis, thus blowing Lucas Steiner's cover? As the plot thickens, and friction escalates between the characters, the film becomes more tense, often frustratingly so, as it reaches its climax.

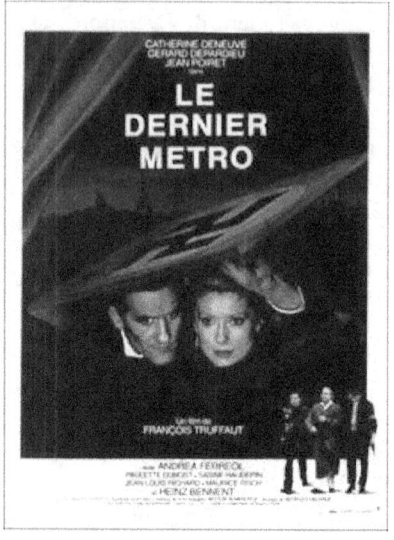

Though Jules and Jim is often picked out as Truffaut's long lasting masterpiece, his seminal offering to the world, I personally believe The Last Metro deserves more credit. He had wanted to make a film on the French occupation for some time, having been inspired by both the memoirs of actor Jean Marais, and his own uncle and grandfather, who were both caught during the actual era when they were smuggling messages across borders. Truffaut went looking for actors in September of 1979, immediately thinking of Catherine Deneuve as Marion, for whom he wrote the part. When Deneueve agreed to play the role, Truffaut knew he had to cast a formidable actor opposite her, someone who could create believable tension and embody the more Jack the Lad traits of Bernard. He knew Depardieu was the man for the job, but it took some time to convince Gerard to sign up, for he was initially unconvinced that he would enjoy working with Francois, as he admitted he did not like his style. Eventually however, and thankfully, Depardieu was won over.

The fact Depardieu came on board was vital to the success of the film, for it is hard to imagine the film working, or the tension between Bernard and Marion being so convincing, without Gerard's rustic edginess. Deneuve, as appealing as ever, is both radiant and beautiful as

Marion, a wonderful characterisation of a powerful, steadfast woman who is also a star of the stage and screen. Playing an actress from another era must be a challenge, but Deneuve pulls it off, playing a woman who is already a myth of the silver screen and pulls in the punters. Her sexiness, as Lucas becomes a strange hermetic father-like figure in her life, is matched by Gerard's slight air of unpredictability and danger. Here is an actor of inspired spontaneity and magic at his early best.

Truffaut establishes true suspense, but resists Hitchcockian techniques and manipulated tension, denying the fall back on dramatic music, conventional scenes of snooping Nazis only just missing sight of their Jewish man-on-the-run. The Last Metro is remarkable because it is gripping and full of tension, but it never resorts to clichés and familiarities. It's simply a good story, establishing believable and likeable (in some cases, detestable) characters who you care about in the trust sense. This is where the film becomes compulsively watchable, having you on the end of your seat, not due to the application of well practised film techniques, but straight forward story telling.

The Last Metro is a truly immaculate film, as close to perfect as you could get. It's a rich and rewarding experience which boasts wonderful, grounded performances, stunning sets and beautiful costumes. It is a masterwork in the truest sense, thanks to the wonderful cast, but most of all for Truffaut's assured control of the whole piece.

It was a big hit in Truffaut's native France as well as over the world, particularly in America, where it made three million dollars in profit. It won ten awards at the Cesars, including Best Picture, while Truffaut won Best Director and Deneuve and Depardieu were rewarded for their fine acting. It also garnered nominations for Best Foreign Language Film at the Oscars and the Golden Globes.

Reviews were almost universally glowing. Though Roger Ebert found it overly involved with the goings on of the theatrical sorts and neglectful of the war outside and the presence of the Nazis, he was perhaps missing the point. Truffaut's film is a microcosm of the period, following a group of people ensuring the show goes on despite the world being in turmoil. That is, of course, the point, with the Nazis secondary to the predicaments which the actors - and the director downstairs of course - find themselves facing.

Other critics loved it, with Vincent Canby declaring it at the time as "a dazzlingly subversive work". Deneuve herself once called it the best film she had ever been in. "It's the top of everything in my career. I am very proud to be in that film."

Gerard Depardieu found himself alongside Catherine Deneuve once again in Alain Corneau's gripping Choice of Arms (1981), which also starred his future Jean de Florette co-star Yves Montand. With a sharp script from Alain and co-writer Michel Grisolia, it concerns Noel (Montand), a retired gangster who now cares for horses on his country estate, living an idyllic life with Nicole (Deneuve), his beautiful wife. Meanwhile, three crooks appear to be in a spot of trouble, and after attracting the attention of the police, the wildest of the three, Mickey (Depardieu) shoots a cop dead. Going into an abandoned wasteland, their car is besieged by bullets from a rival criminal. The third crook flees, leaving only Mickey and the older Serge. After injuring Serge, the gun man gets away, and Mickey and Serge end up at Noel's home, Serge recuperating in one of the spare beds. But through no fault of his own, Noel becomes entangled in a murky plot, the kind of which he thought he had left behind him in his long gone crime days. The police turn up at Noel's house, so Mickey hides out in Paris with a friend, but he accuses Noel of informing on him. It is here where things turn particularly nasty.

Choice of Arms is a compelling crime thriller, with a healthy pace, suspense and plenty of tension, but in true European fashion it is not exploitative, violent for the sake of it or cliché ridden. It is, in fact, an in-depth character study of what people will reduce themselves to, an exploration of humanity in the truest sense. It is, therefore, a film to enjoy for the performances, even if the plot itself is engaging.

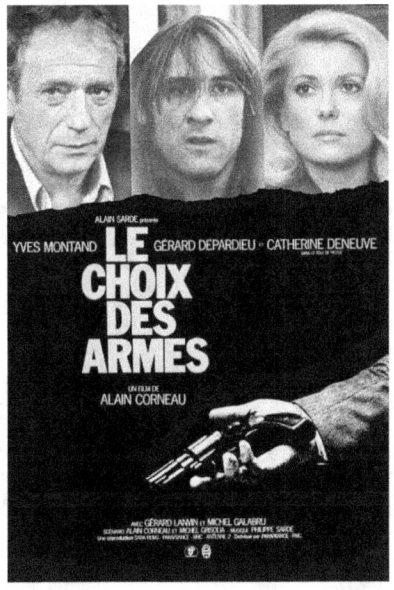

Montand, a true icon of French cinema, is solid as Noel, a self assured man seeing his paradise slipping away with the arrival of these two unwanted, shady characters, while the gorgeous Deneuve is as effective as ever, perfect as a calm wife who personifies, with her smooth exterior and gentle way, the fact that Noel's life had certainly improved since giving up the gangster life.

One of the most stylish and original entries in the vampire horror genre is Tony Scott's 1983 cult favourite, The Hunger. Initially both a commercial and critical disappointment, it's built up a following down the years and today has its own set of loyal defenders. The film stars Deneuve as a glamorous and sexy vampire named Miriam, who has been alive for thousands of years and has had various partners by her side down the centuries. She promises them immortality and endless life; and though they do enjoy a long run, all of a sudden each of her lovers ages and crumbles away. In 1980s New York (London in fact, where Scott and the crew shot most of the picture) she is living with John (David Bowie), who has been her companion since the 18th century, and together they prowl the night for fresh blood. They kill their victims with Ankh pendants which double as small blades ideal for slicing open a jugular vein, then dispose of the bodies in their basement furnace. They are happy together in their quiet, hermetic life. Suddenly however, John begins to age, and rather quickly too. After seeing a gerontologist named Dr Sarah Roberts on the TV, John pays her a visit to discuss some prematurely aged apes she is studying. When she stands him up, John leaves, but Sarah will not be deterred. She later visits Miriam and John's home, only Miriam has placed the crumbling, ailing man in a coffin. Miriam now sets her sights on Sarah and making her the latest companion in her journey through everlasting life.

The Hunger was firstly criticised for being overly stylised, shot as it was by Tony Scott, a veteran of the advertising world. Many critics felt the film had little beneath its glossy, arty surface, while Bowie himself commented in the press that, while it looked good, there was definitely too much explicit gore. The film, quite naturally of course, is rather bloody, and indeed Scott veers off into over the top direction now and then, but The Hunger can best be enjoyed for its engaging plot and strong performances.

Bowie is fantastic as the concerned John, desperately hanging on to his life but seeing it ebb away by the minute. Unfortunately he is missing for the second half of the film, but thankfully Susan Sarandon is excellent as Miriam's latest target. Deneuve however is the one who holds it all together, with a graceful and elegant performance which keeps the film grounded. Amidst all the camera trickery, creepy music and neck biting, Deneuve remains grounded in a weird kind of reality, classy as ever in her exotic costumes and laid back manners. In truth she makes the film, and it's impossible to imagine the whole thing without her.

There were other highlights in the 80s. In **Let's Hope It's a Girl** (1986) she was directed by Mario Monicelli in an Italian production, alongside Bernard Blier and Philippe Noiret. A hidden gem in Deneuve's filmography, it concerns a family in Tuscany who after a falling out bid to relocate to Rome. This warm and appealing picture is one of the finest Italian films of the 80s (up there with Ettore Scola's work in the decade) and deserves a discovery.

In Scene of the Crime (1986) she found herself in another family predicament, only a much more serious one. It follows a young boy who, traumatised by the divorce of his parents, is visited by a fugitive who's escaped from prison. Deneuve plays the boy's mother Lili, who is stuck in a rut running a night club. This is one of her more surprising, multi faceted performances, a powerful effort that reveals the depth of her range and commitment to a part.

A Strange Place to Meet (1988), known in France as Drole d'endroit pour une rencontre, is one of those rare gems that, for one reason or another, has unfortunately disappeared into obscurity. Directed by Francois Dupeyron, from a script co written with Dominique Faysse, it's a beautifully acted drama of unfulfilled desire and indifference.

The plot, or the outline at least, concerns Catherine Deneuve (seemingly more beautiful as she got into her forties) having an argument with her husband - or as we are told - while he is driving them down a frantic highway. When he nearly runs over a mad woman who rushes into the middle of the road, he swerves the car off to one side, stops and ends up throwing Deneuve out into the night, leaving her there and driving off into the darkness. At the road side is Gerard Depardieu, a surgeon having some car trouble, claiming he has been there for to days trying to fix the engine. At first irritated by Deneuve's presence, given she insists on waiting there for the husband she insists will return to pick her up, he develops a strange infatuation for her, masochistically pushing her away through the night, alienating her, and then trying to win her over. She sleeps in Depardieu's car and wakes in the morning to frantically ask the other sleeping drivers in the lay-by if they have seen her husband. They answer no, but undeterred by the rejection, she refuses to leave and insists he will come back for her.

Eventually Depardieu convinces her to come with him to a nearby cafe, where he hilariously fusses over choosing the right table where they can have their morning coffee and sandwiches. Tensions develop, with Depardieu clearly developing a crush on, if not an obsession with this strange woman who would wait a year for a man never intending to return. She on the other hand, could not care less for Depardieu as a possible romantic distraction, irritated by his heavy handedness and ineptness with women. They stay at the cafe another full day and night, coming across all types of people; these include a woman who agrees to sell Deneuve the outfit she is wearing, because it reminds her of one she used to wear for her husband in happier times; and a group of crude, hard drinking truckers, one of whom spends the night with Deneuve, pulling the curtains closed on the window to his truck as Depardieu, sitting across in his car, reacts with the extreme jealousy of a bitter husband. What will become of Deneuve and Depardieu, the obsessed and the object of the obsession?

A Strange Place to Meet is a play put to film, a series of unfolding events which border on the surreal, the absurd, and are often plain funny and strangely farcical. Depardieu puts in a complex, multi faceted performance as a man in love but also a slave to his own uselessness with the fairer sex. Deneuve is magnificent, striking as ever of course, but portraying a muddled, confused, put upon, if not totally mad woman. There is an air of mystery about her, with certain behavioural traits suggesting the husband is not a husband at all, maybe a boyfriend, perhaps something else. Some have even said she may be a lady of the night, one in the throes of madness, lamenting a husband that does not even exist. Either way, whether a crazed enigma or unhappy wife, slowly being dropped on to the rubbish heap, Depardieu is besotted, yet tortured by her disinterest.

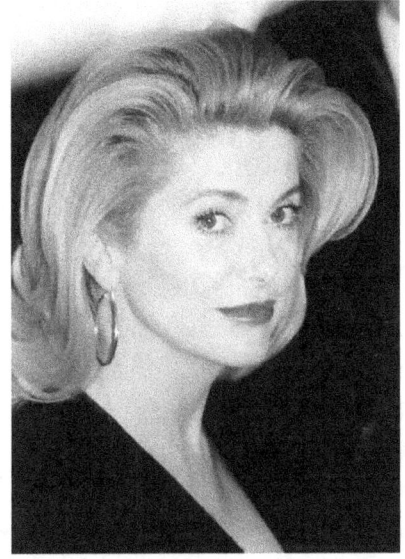

The most interesting dynamic here, between two of French cinema's brightest lights, is the fact that Deneuve is desperate for love and acceptance, but attempting to earn it from a man who couldn't care less. Perversely, Depardieu is the same, hungry if not starving for Deneuve's love, but getting shunned heartlessly.

Neither can see the truth before them, blinded as they are by their ignorance and love induced madness; Deneuve with a man who would drop everything for her, Depardieu faced with a woman denying him every step of the way.

Curiously, Dupeyron does not make this a beautiful film. Even though I viewed an old VHS, it was clear to me that Dupeyron was not concerned with aesthetics, but tension, atmosphere and a certain raw reality. The camera stays on the characters in long takes, angles are straight forward, never fussy, and emphasis at all times is on man and woman; Deneuve and Depardieu, the spaces between them, the gaps which cannot be filled. The only real artful shot, repeated a few times through the long nights, is of a wispy mist drifting silently over the moon. This is a film to watch for the performances, and thankfully the director takes a step back and allows the two legends to do their work. They are marvellous from beginning to end.

It was greeted warmly upon release and is regarded highly by those in the know. Tine Out wrote: "Talk about minimal: Dupeyron's feature debut is a road movie where they only travel 10 kilometres. Deneuve's in the throes of a very heavy, possibly masochistic relationship with the man who dumped her; Depardieu is a lonely, romantic doctor who's doggedly hopeless with the opposite sex. Nothing is entirely resolved, tempting hints about the characters' lives aren't elaborated upon (*is* she married, mad, or a high class hooker?), and the film retains the haunting inconsequentiality of a chance encounter. The romantic protestations, set against the grim background of a plastic café, are poignant and dreamlike, the characters are drifters seeking refuge or escape, and the whole film is comic and bitter-sweet."

The New York Times however found it frustrating, perhaps confused by the lack of explanations and solutions, with Janet Maslin writing the following: "For neophyte acting students, this material might seem worth playing to the hilt, but for two of the French cinema's greatest stars it's an odd choice indeed. The reasons why Mr. Depardieu and Miss Deneuve chose to co-produce A Strange Place to Meet will be, for anyone who sees the film, a complete mystery. Among the more absurd touches here, beyond the sight of Miss Deneuve wandering dazedly around a truck stop in her dark glasses and sable, are the fact that Mr. Depardieu is supposed to be a surgeon and the peculiar identification that Miss Deneuve's character feels with a woman who has, at the beginning of the story, tried to jump in front of her car."

For me, the fact that Depardieu and Deneuve chose this abstract material proved they were happy to take risks, to go against the star system and choices expected of them. Admirers of the two leads will find A Strange Place to Meet an absolute delight, a film not afraid to go off track, dwell on minor details and go

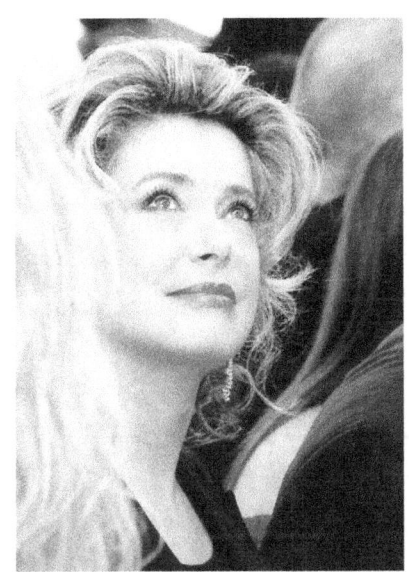

and Catherine's performance in it is definitely among her finest efforts.

She plays Elaine, the owner of a plantation during the French Indochina era of the 30s to the 50s. She has an adopted daughter named Camille, who she takes in when the girl's biological parents die in a crash, and continues to run her father's rubber business. An epic tale in the truest sense, Elaine and Camille's life during this period is told against the uprising against the French colonies in Vietnam.

on side tangents. Refreshingly ragged in style, the lack of technique and reliance on frilly camera work makes more room for these two towering talents, playing the kind of characters you might meet in a strange dream, rather than on the big screen.

Indochine received a wide release and much acclaim, even winning Best Foreign Film at the Oscars. Deneuve herself, though not bagging the Academy Award, did earn the Cesar that year. Even when reviews of the film were critical, Deneuve earned high praise. In the New York Times for instance, it was written that "Catherine Deneuve reigns in Indochine. That is, she presides over its second-rate fiction with the manner of an empress who knows her powers are constitutionally limited but who continues to take her

Of all her work, the one she gives in Indochine (1992) is perhaps her most acclaimed performance, and the one - if it truly matters - which won her an Oscar nomination. Indochine remains a powerful film duties seriously. She can't change the course of the film, but her lofty presence keeps it from flying apart."

Despite such petty reviews, the film was lauded in her native France and was a huge hit there.

Fresh off her success in Indochine, Deneuve went on to other remarkable films, such as My Favourite Season (1993), in which she played a woman who, with her estranged brother, begins to care for her ailing mother. It was another critical and box office hit for her. The performance, though not as celebrated as the one she gave in Indochine, was just as strong.

She received wide acclaim and a Cesar nomination for her work in Place Vendome (1998), a stylish and slick thriller from Nicole Garcia. She plays the run down wife of a diamond merchant who has committed suicide. A former jeweller herself, who quit the job and turned to booze, she takes over the business and realises she has inherited more than she bargained for.

Though Place Vendome is quite a cold film (purposely of course), Deneuve is not playing a standard former alcoholic; this role is complex and Deneuve brings believability to a part which could have come across as clichéd. Though the film itself is not always the best it could be, Deneuve is undeniably fabulous.

She was also a vital part of Paul Ruiz's version of Proust's In Search of Lost Time, the award winning Time Regained (1999). The film, a slow and reflective poem on life and death, is a visual and intellectual treat, though anyone thinking it might be a good way into Deneuve's filmography may be mistaken. Still, it is an essential French film of the 1990s.

As is East/West (1999), Deneuve's final film of the decade, in which she plays an actress in a plot involving Russian exiles being invited back by Stalin after the end of the Second World War. Working again for Indochine director Regis Wargnier, Deneuve is formidably strong throughout.

One of the highest profile films Deneuve has ever appeared in is Dancer in the Dark (2000), Lars Von Trier's imaginative and highly original musical. It stars Bjork as a factory worker called Selma. While working in her demanding 9 to 5 job, she has to contend with a serious degenerative eye condition. Slaving away to save up for an operation which may cure her, Selma is also hoping her beloved son does not go down the same route. Catherine Deneuve has a key supporting role as Kathy, a fellow worker and close friend of Selma's.

The final part in Trier's Golden Heart Trilogy, it is a film which looks like no other. Given a large budget, the shoot itself was rather ambitious, as recalled by Deneuve in her published film diaries, and at points was a turbulent set. It was filmed on hand held digital cameras, unusual for the time, and therefore immediately has a documentary feel to it. This was vital to Trier's vision. Bjork however, did not enjoy the experience. Later she said that she found the picture so demanding she vowed never to take a starring role in a film ever again, though later still corrected herself and said that she had never wished to act and signed up quite simply because Von Trier was an exception. Either way, I feel Bjork puts in a very effective performance, even if she wasn't a natural and found the work itself taxing. (She later made serious claims against Von Trier, but such controversy is perhaps for elsewhere.)

Deneuve's part, I feel, could have been bigger, but we are graced with some beautiful acting from the Grand Dame herself. In her diary she highlights her confusion at some of von Trier's technique, as well as Bjork's behaviour, but she manages to pull out a decent effort, even if she does clearly look bemused at times.

Dancer in the Dark came at a time when Bjork was at her most popular, so naturally the film attracted a lot of attention. It was a sizeable box office hit (especially for an art film) but received mixed reviews.

Roger Ebert loved the movie but highlighted the polarising views. He wrote "Some reasonable people will admire Lars von Trier's Dancer in the Dark, and others will despise it. An excellent case can be made for both positions. Dancer in the Dark is not like any other movie at the multiplex this week, or this year. It is not a well made film, is not in good taste, is not plausible or, for many people, entertaining. But it smashes down the walls of habit that surround so many movies. It returns to the wellsprings. It is a bold, reckless gesture. And since Bjork has announced that she will never make another movie, it is a good thing she sings."

On the other end, Peter Bradshaw detested the film, writing in the Guardian, "For its sheer effrontery, for its browbeating melodrama and pseudo-tragedy, Lars von Trier's Dancer in the Dark has to be the most sensationally silly film of the year - as well as the most shallow and crudely manipulative. Everything about it is silly." Of Deneuve's presence, he wrote

"Selma's best friend in the factory is played by Catherine Deneuve, in full Marie Antoinette milkmaid mode, sporting a humble overcoat, a headscarf, and a French accent you could slice a baguette with. What is this haughty patrician exquisite doing here? God only knows. Von Trier appears to have roped them together as if for an art installation."

Nevertheless, Dancer in the Dark was awarded the Palme d'Or at Cannes Film Festival and Bjork won Best Actress. It also garnered nominations at the Oscars and the Cesars, while also bagging Best Foreign Language Film at the Independent Spirit Awards. Twenty years on it may not be as remembered as one might have thought, but Dancer in the Dark is still held in high esteem and is worthy of being rediscovered by younger film buffs.

8 Women (2002) is in my view one of the very best pictures Deneuve has ever been in. Written and directed by Francois Ozon, this all star gem was a huge box office hit upon release and

nearly twenty years since it was made, is as vibrant and colourful as ever.

Deneuve plays a mother who, at Christmas, is expecting certain relatives round for festivities. Just as people start to arrive, her husband, Marcel, is found dead in bed with a knife in his back, and the film speedily turns into a murder mystery full of twists and turns, not to mention unexpected song and dance routines.

Deneuve is excellent as the woman in denial, who until now has glided through life ignoring the uglier side of her husband and life in general. She is aided by the other actresses too, in particular the wonderful Fanny Ardent as her street walking sister in law, Isabelle Huppert as a buttoned up sister and Emmanuelle Beart as the maid who is not all she appears to be.

Deservedly so, the whole cast received the Golden Bear at the Berlin Film Festival, and along with its healthy box office it garnered strong reviews. Some, including the San Francisco Chronicle, dubbed it a masterpiece, while typically Entertainment Weekly yearned for an American remake.

Sharply scripted, superbly played and wonderfully put together, 8 Women is an essential entry in Deneuve's 21st century filmography.

A year later, Deneuve worked for the third time with Manoel de Oliveira (after The Convent in 1995 and I'm Going Home in 01) in A Talking Picture (2003), opposite john Malkovich. A slow, carefully placed picture (in true Manoel de Oliveira style) it's another gem from the singular de Oliveira and should definitely be sought out.

A Christmas Tale (2008) is serious competition for being the best film Catherine Deneuve has been in during her productive and prolific run in the 21st century. Written and directed by Arnaud Desplechin, it's an ambitious, long, but never sprawling family story set during the festive period. She and Jean Paul Roussillon play the heads of a family. Deneuve is Junon, a strong woman who finds out she has a rare form of cancer and in order to survive needs the bone marrow of a biological match. The film begins just as they are all about to come together at the grand old house, with Roussillon as Abel, the kind and patient father keeping things together.

This multi layered, wonderfully scripted film boasts superb performances. Deneuve is fantastic of course, the backbone of the film in many ways, while the children are played by some of France's best actors; Henri, the wild and untamed one, is played excellently by Mathieu Amalric, while Chaira Mastroianni (Deneuve's daughter to Marcello Mastroianni) is excellent as Sylvia.

If you were to judge the film by its title and DVD cover, you might expect a heart-warming family tale set during the Christmas period. The film, of course, is nothing of the sort; it's a relatable and realistic study of a family pulling in different directions, one full of spats and petty quarrelling, back stabbing and bitchiness. If we are all honest, it's a little too much like reality.

Arnaud holds it all together with assured direction, floating amidst the varied activity unobtrusively, like an observer amongst the family seeing it all unfold. We warm to the characters despite (and in some cases because of) their flaws, and Arnaud makes a brave move in not shying away from unattractive traits and behaviour. It's a truly wonderful film, a master class in acting and direction. It was also Jean Paul Roussillon's final film before he died, in a performance which won him the Best Actor gong at the Cesars.

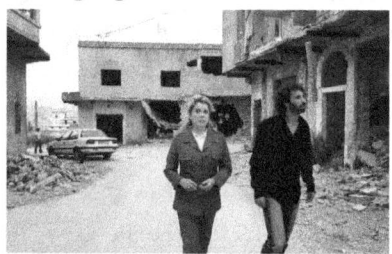

Though Deneuve's filmography is full of experimental and often unusual films, Je Veux Voir (2008) is certainly one of the most unique. Directed by Joana Hadjithomas and Khali Joreige, it fuses documentary, fiction and spontaneity. Deneuve stars as a version of herself, complete with body guard, who arrives in Lebanon where she understands she will be making an experimental film of some kind. She meets with Rabih Mroue, who begins to drive her across war torn Beirut and guide her through the bombed out ruins, speaking of the latest war, the last war and one before that. He takes her through the sad and brick laden suburbs, then to the area where he grew up, though it is a shambolic shadow of its former self and the current state of his grandmother's old home, now a pile of bricks, clearly saddens him.

This strange, unsettling and ultimately brave film runs at just over an hour, and unashamedly shows us the impact of war, on what it can do to a society and individuals. We see it all through the camera yes, at times shaky and unsteady as it should be, but we also see it through the compassionate and very open eyes of Deneuve. When she naps for a moment, we feel as if we have napped with her; when she is terrified during a "fake" air raid, we too feel her terror. This is war and devastation as seen through the gaze of a cinema icon. It is also enjoyable too to observe the interactions she has with Rabih, clearly improvised and very much in the moment.

Deneuve spoke of the film in a 2008 interview with Elle, stating "The subject is Lebanon, just after the war. I first read a short script without dialogues that excited me. I quickly decided to accept, perhaps for fear of changing my mind. Personalities are often asked for their opinions on anything and everything, as if fame were enough to put us in an expert position. I had read passionately the reports on this war, and the articles showed how complex it was and that it was impossible to have a unilateral opinion. I thought the film was a rare opportunity to see with my own eyes being accompanied by absolutely concerned people. As I say in the film, I had no certainty of understanding anything. Doing is always better than talking, even if, finally, I find myself chatting today! I didn't expect to be in such a movie at all. A six-day shoot, very well organized it is true, rarely leads to a feature film. The conversations we hear are ours. We sometimes forgot that we were being filmed. I rarely had the feeling of playing because I was taken by my interest in this trip. It's rare to be entirely united with what you're performing, even if the final, fictional gala scene was written. I, too, wanted to see the destruction, even though the diggers were already starting to rebuild everything."

I can fairly say there is not a wasted shot in this powerful, raw piece of filmmaking, one that may not be quotable, stylish or easy on the eye, but is vitally important and essential viewing for anyone concerned with humanity and the price of war. It gives the viewer a glimpse into a place we have all heard of but may not know the truth about. One thing can you say about this film then, is that it offers a truth, if not an explanation or solution.

Catherine Deneuve then took the lead role in Francois Ozon's Potiche (2010), based on the play by Pierre Barillet and Jean-Pierre Gredy. This stylish adaptation is set in 1977 and stars Deneuve as the wife of a well off factory owner who suddenly gets to take over the business when the workers rise up against him. After being suppressed and belittled by him through their whole marriage, it is now her turn to blossom and show the world and herself what she was capable of all along. She thrives in the job and in turn realises what her husband truly is.

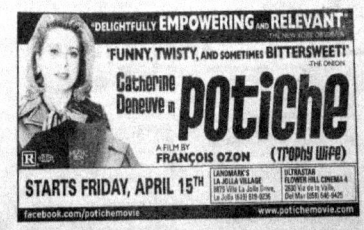

Ozon had wanted to make the film for ten years after first seeing the play, and lifted inspiration from the films of Jacques Demy in style and presentation (it has much of the colour, passion and liveliness of Demy's work, but not the haunted melancholia), making it somewhat of a dream for him that he was able to cast Deneuve, who, it has to be said, carries the picture throughout. As wonderfully designed it may be, in costume and backdrop, it is Deneuve who is the film's backbone, delivering one of her liveliest and sharpest turns of the last few years. Deservedly so, she was nominated for a Cesar, though she did not win. Credit must also go to the brilliant Gerard Depardieu, who plays the mayor who assists Deneuve in the heated strikes, who also turns out to be an old flame who strikes up new passion in Deneuve.

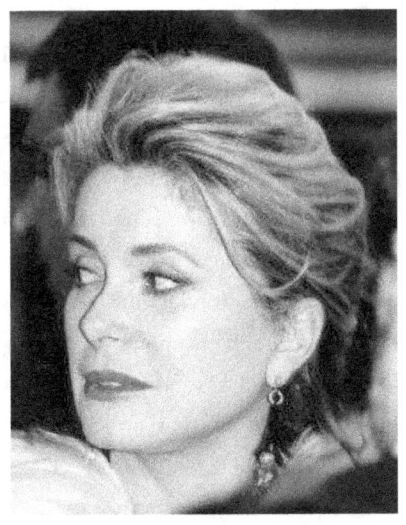

Potiche was both a critical and box office hit upon release, making back nearly 30 million on its 12 million budget, and garnering solid reviews the world over.

The Hollywood Reporter boasted of a "masterful central performance by grande dame Catherine Deneuve as an oppressed bourgeois housewife who finds liberation. Though her transformation from mouse to lion is a foregone conclusion, Deneuve never loses the audience for a minute. Her change of clothes and hair-styles from scene to scene is a laugh in itself. What the audience cheers for, though, is her final, triumphant combo of professionality and ageless femininity. Not only does she get the best of all the men, whose pretentious sexism is mercilessly lampooned; she ends up as the happiest person in the picture."

Though set over forty years ago, Ozon's bubbly farce feels modern and not simply a stylistic return to the past. This is a film that is relevant now, regardless of the vibrant seventies colours, but vitally due to Deneuve's charismatic performance and her inspiring escape from that prison of a marriage.

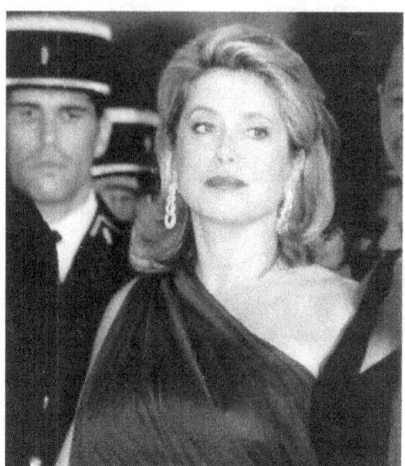

It has been said that Deneuve's roles have been less icy, much warmer in recent years. One interviewer brought this up to her in 2010 and she had her own view: "I supposed it's called life, you know? Time. And experience. I think you have certain barriers that fall after a time, and as you go further in age, things peel off that allow you to be more open. You fear less. It doesn't mean you have no fear, but you fear less. Also the life I had, the children I have - my relation to people is quite protective."

And Deneuve has continued, too, to challenge herself and her audience. Beloved (2011) had her once again beside her daughter Chiara, in a story that spanned thirty years. Light and airy, the film is great fun and has a rhythmic atmosphere to it, rather like Demy's work, though perversely it is not a musical.

On My Way (2013) was a chance for her to reflect and play a very full role, that of a woman who goes out on the road, leaving her muddled, messy life behind her. She earned yet another Cesar nomination, though in truth the performance was so good, so well observed and subtly poignant that if there was any justice she would have earned every award going.

Most recently, Deneuve was alongside Juliette Binoche and Ethan Hawke in the wonderful The Truth (2019), in which she plays an ageing legendary actress who has just published her memoir, much to the horror of her daughter. Here, Deneuve is playing with her own image, but in truth the character is also far from Deneuve, famously modest and low key in real life. Still, the role shows she is not sailing smoothly on her reputation and is still not afraid of taking risks.

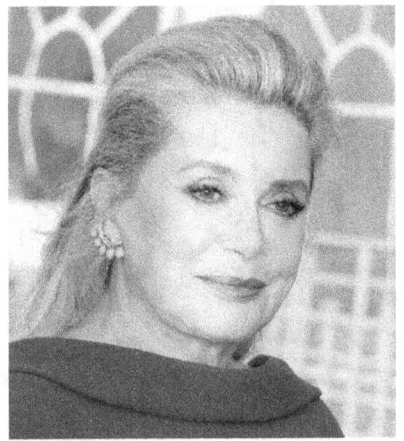

It might be a cliché to say that Deneuve is having one hell of a run lately (or she was at least, before COVID), but it's also true. She has never, in all honesty, had a dip, but the last decade or so has been terrific and perhaps unmatched by any film actress in history. She is also receiving a lot of honours, which worries her. "Tributes, they start at the time when things seem to be slowing down. You have to be careful with what they call an homage, a tribute, because it becomes something very final."

Deneuve, who once said cinema was her life and passion, is as in love with the medium as ever before. She clearly adores life on a film set and the collaborations that come about when making a picture. What is extraordinary though is the fact that not only does she still look very much like the famous and glamorous Deneuve, even into her mid seventies, but she is just as powerful on screen as ever, and I honestly cannot think of anyone else I can say that about and be telling the truth.

"These days I am treated like an institution," she said, "I'm very aware of that and very careful."

She's a one off, and shows no signs of slowing or weakening. The only question I have is one of excitement: What's next?

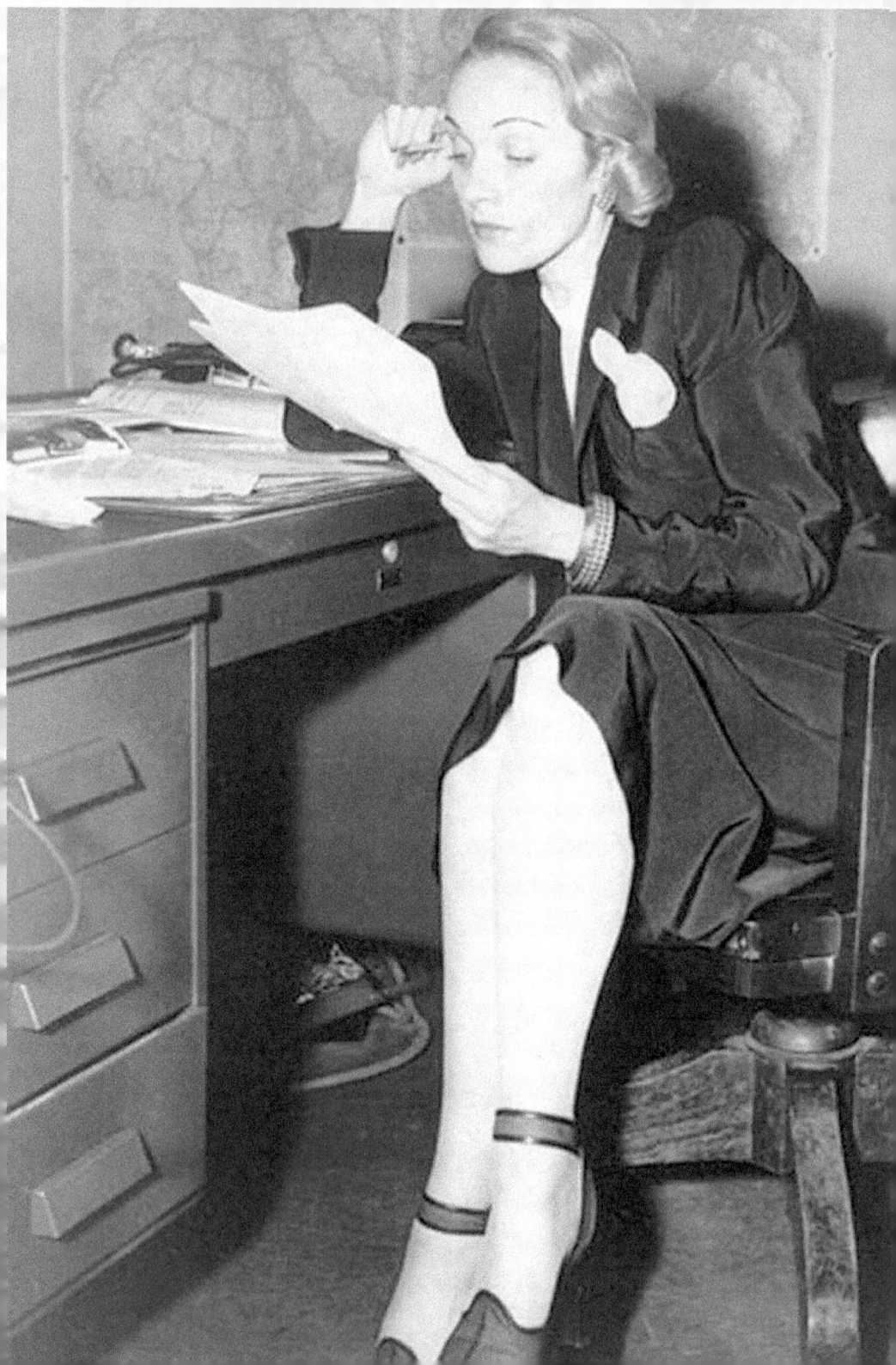

PETER RIVA ON HIS GRANDMOTHER
MARLENE DIETRICH

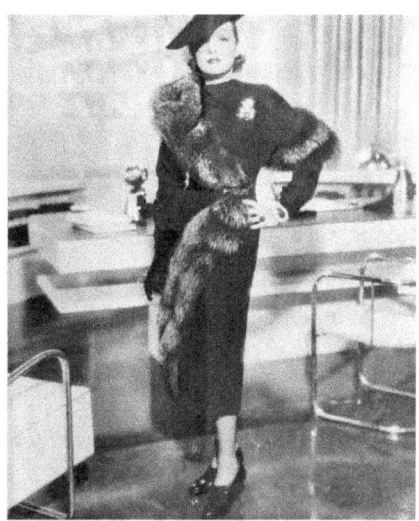

Peter Riva runs the official Marlene Dietrich website. Here he recalls fond memories of his grandmother.

Is it hard for people to understand just how famous Marlene was all over the world?

Not really, as her films still play and many, many fans still feel she is alive and real... Film has that effect, more than TV.

She pushed so many boundaries in her films in the early thirties. How do you think Marlene was seen and perceived in comparison to other starlets of the time? I feel her work has aged the best of all.

She understood the medium. The less you gesticulate, the more you make the eye and camera focus on her stillness, the more her 4 meter high image would convince. It is that honesty to the eye that remains.

What are your earliest memories of your grandmother? This may be a huge question, but is there anything specific you can mention?

I was born in 1950, so I had 40+ years with her as a grandmother and a relative who was talented, demanding (of excellence), and to be shared with the world. Earliest

53

memory (other than visual memory)... Mike and I got the measles when my mother was pregnant in '57, so she took over the household – and 100% immediate observance of her commands was essential – always given with encouragement to do the right thing.

Having such a larger than life figure as a grandma fascinates me. When she was with the family was there a massive difference to the public Dietrich persona? And did she turn that on and off at will?

A phone call, a visitor come to talk business, she would change from grandmother (Massy) to Marlene. Mike and I learned that early.

You've spoken of her kindness to you and her nurturing. What are some of your favourite aspects of her when you were growing up?

She was never unkind or cruel, even if I goofed. Disciplinarian? Yes, sure, but not with punishment. You just

wanted to do it right to please her. And what do you buy such a world star for Christmas? I paid attention and saw she liked green ink ballpoints in the last '50s... so I bought a dozen Bic ballpoint green ink pens (hard to find in NY!)... and she was genuinely thrilled.

How much do you think her childhood formed who she became, and those early years in a very different Germany?

She was Prussian elite class and her manners, dedication to "flicht" were part of her backbone. Her father's brother was von Dietrich, he was the second son and found a job in the royal household (what people today mistakenly call "policeman"). Once a true lady, always a true lady.

By your mother's fantastic book, I am equally fascinated by her final years. Did you see her much in this era? I also find it moving that she wanted to preserve the Dietrich image and

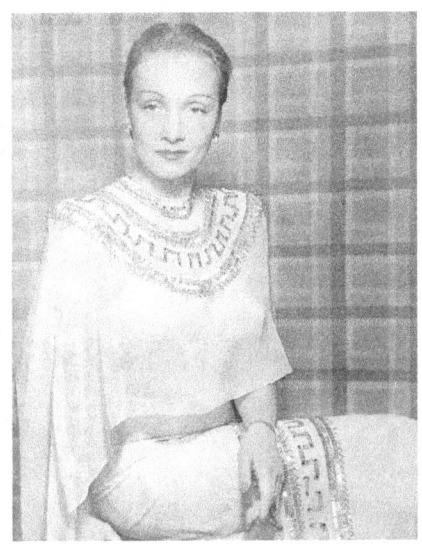

keep her in people's minds as she once had been.

Sandra (my wife) and I saw her a few times a year, spoke on the phone at least weekly. Anything she wanted from London (where we lived) we found and sent. She made the best skate (la raie) in aspic you ever tasted and made it and sent it by mail often. Visiting her at 12 Ave. Montaigne was always a pleasure for us all, we'd have lunch, discuss my mother and father, brothers, and leave her before nightfall.

Do you think her films, especially the marvellous ones with von Sternberg, and then A Foreign Affair, Stage Fright and all those classics, often get unfairly overlooked in favour of her image alone? I really do feel she had a much larger range than people imagine and think she was a very fine actor.

She only "acted" three times as star: Blue Angel, Judgement at Nurnberg and A Touch of Evil (see the director's cut only!). In all her other films she PERFORMED "Dietrich" as she was asked to do. A professional, without any ego or vanity whatsoever, the job, her responsibility, allowed her to perform faultlessly. As an actor, her performance in A Touch of Evil is brilliant. Of course, Witness for the Prosecution also had an almost cameo acting role, but at the time it was a kept secret in Hollywood (why she was not nominated). My favourite movie of my grandmother (playing herself) was No Highway... 100% Massy.

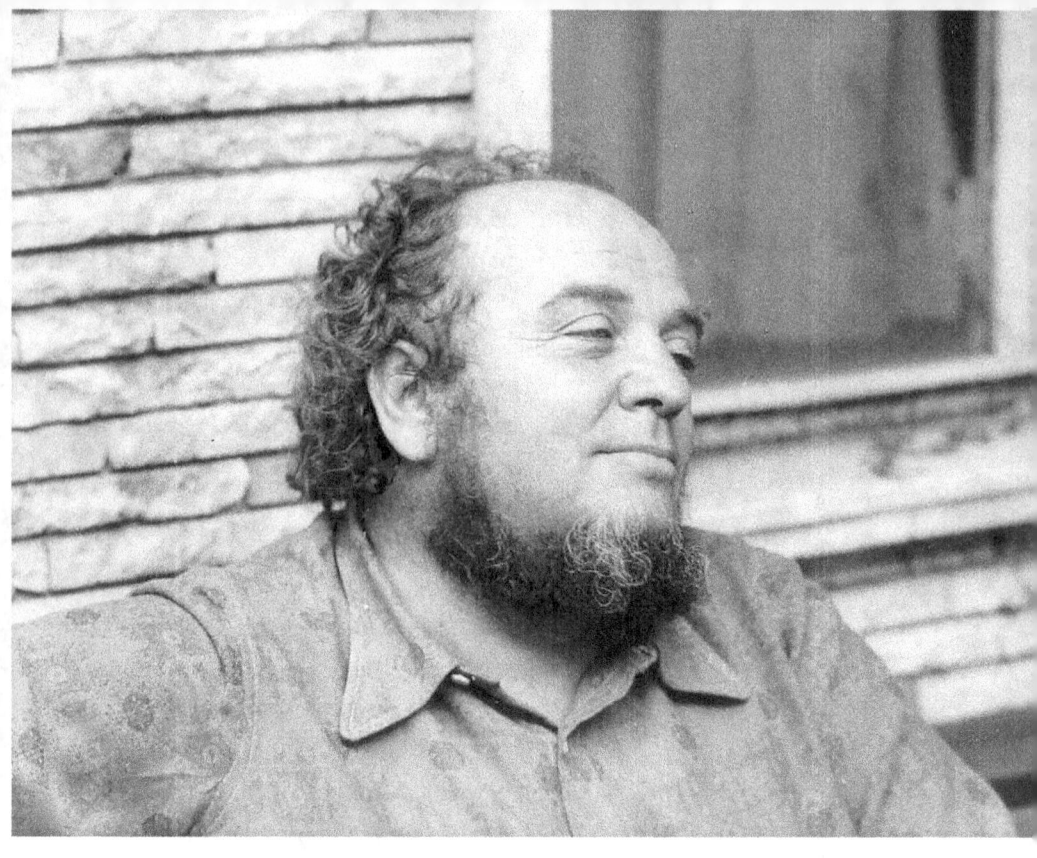

MARCO FERRERI HIS FILMS IN THE 1970s

While his name might not predominantly pop up when modern critics, especially those outside Italy, are discussing the maestros of Italian cinema, Marco Ferreri was one of the most outrageous, unique and brilliant filmmakers of his generation. Ferreri's films, often grotesque, often very funny and always compulsively watchable, are not easy to categorise today. Though he often found himself equally criticised and applauded, Ferreri was the kind of man who refused to bow down and make the kind of film many wished he had. Most famous today for seminal classics like Dillinger is Dead (1969) and the hedonistic masterpiece La Grande Bouffe (1973), Ferreri's full oeuvre is one to behold, making it a shame indeed that some of his work is so hard to track down or remains unavailable commercially to a potential audience who would lap up his satirical, hard edged style of expressionism.

Ferreri, born in Milan in May of 1928, first trained to be a vet, but found his interest soon turning to cinema. At first finding it hard to get the ball rolling, he sold lenses and camera equipment to make a living, then sold liquor and found work as a journalist. He shot commercials early on and also worked on several Italian films, sometimes as an uncredited script contributor. Frustrated with his lack of progress, Ferreri moved to Spain, where he made his earliest films, like El Pisto (1958), before relocating back to Italy for his satires

on married life and relationships, like The Conjugal Bed (1963). In 1964 he scored a success with The Ape Woman (1964) which established him as a major force. Still, he pushed things further with Dillinger is Dead (1969), largely thought to be his finest film. Starring Michel Piccoli as a man experiencing alienation one long night, during which he finds an antique gun and paints it up ornately, it was a tale of enclosure, isolation and the self. It was in complete contrast to the next film of his which caused as big a stir, if not more controversy; 1973's La Grande Bouffe, about a group of privileged middle aged men gorging themselves to death. Though Ferreri was adamant it was not an anti consumerist film, it is largely read as such and does seem to be a statement, whether he wished it to be or not, on mindless excess and empty greed.

Though it could be said he never made a better, more assured film as La Grande Bouffe, everything he directed afterwards was a grand statement, impossible to ignore or

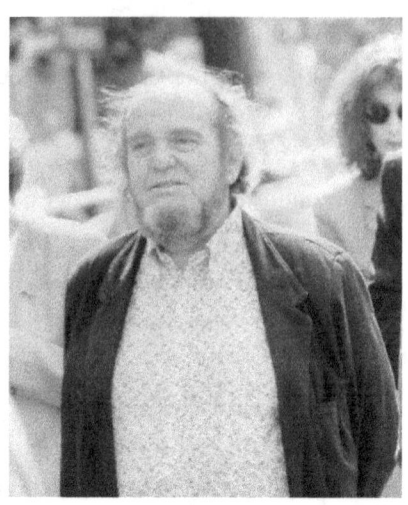

dismiss; his anti American surreal western Don't Touch the White Woman (1974); the ode to manliness, the brilliant Bye Bye Monkey (1978); Tales of Ordinary Madness (1981), based on the work of Charles Bukowski; all the way to 1993's Diary of a Maniac, the last film he made that made a serious splash.

Ferreri died at the relatively young age of 68 in 1997, leaving behind a formidable if daunting filmography. Characterising himself as both a feminist and a misogynist, many modern viewers may find Ferreri's work hopelessly un-PC, if not downright shocking. But if you can get past the fact they were made in a very different time, and were satirical, surrealistic and often symbolic of a greater picture, Ferreri's colourful, vibrant and fearless work will enlighten you.

"I ask women to make for me a portrait of a woman and they always portray to me the Virgin Mary. So misogynist is not a word that makes sense. I think women are stronger than men. They represent the fantastic imagination side of men. I am always speaking as a European, not as an American."

On the other hand, his work remains relevant in that it questions and confronts the system. Speaking in the 1980s, Ferreri said "I have always been political. I thought that I could do it my way. I consider all my films political." On the other hand Ferreri was a man who raised objections, asked questions but never once attempted to provide an answer or solution to the chaos of life. In 1977 he said "The values that once existed no longer exist. The family, the bourgeoisie -- I'm talking about values, morals, economic relationships. They no longer serve a purpose. My films are reactions translated into images." The mourning of these values exists in all his work.

Ferreri did undoubtedly use graphic imagery to get a reaction, but as he himself was reacting against the horrors, injustices and corrupt nature of life itself, he could defend his imagery as an embodied reflection. "Doesn't life shock you enough? The shock I show is no bigger than the shock we see in daily living."

With the themes he explored and the often avant garde approach to putting his messages across, one would presume that Ferreri worked underground with small names. But this was not the cast. Lest we forget, he worked often with Marcello Mastroianni, perhaps the biggest name in world cinema, as well as Michel Piccoli, Ugo Tognazzi, Gerard Depardieu and Philipe Noiret. He won acclaim and major awards, like the Cannes Film Festival Critics'

Prize and Berlin's Golden Bear gong. Today it would be impossible for such a daring, cutting edge filmmaker to attract such big names and garner such mainstream attention.

This article acts as a rough guide through his film work of the 1970s, when he was given full reign it seems to explore the wildest side of his imagination. He had of course made great films before the 1970s and would certainly do again, but it is well understood that this decade was Ferreri's golden period.

L'UDIENZA (1971)

L'Udienza is a transitional piece for Ferreri, the story of a young man who visits Rome with a view of visiting the pope. The Vatican itself is made to look like a soulless cavern, lacking in humanity. Lightly surreal, and with a superb cast that includes Michel Piccoli, Claudia Cardinale and Ugo Tognazzi, it feels in some ways like a build up to his stronger, more defined and assured work of the mid to later seventies. That said, it is still a very enjoyable and thought provoking picture from the alternative maestro of Italian cinema.

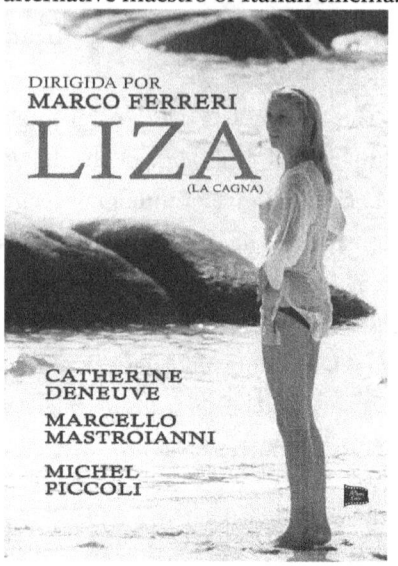

LIZA (1971)

Known across the world as Liza and Love to Eternity, but in Italy as La Cagna (The Bitch), it was the second pairing of Catherine Deneuve and Marcello Mastroianni, and another chance for him to work with one of his favourite directors, the great Ferreri. This time Marcello plays a painter named Giorgio who lives on an island, all alone with his faithful hound. One day his life is interrupted by the arrival of the beautiful Liza (Deneuve), and the pair begin an affair. The relationship between Giorgio and Liza is masochistic and dangerous, and Marco does not shy away from comparing this romance to the bond between a man and his dog. When the dog dies, it is then that she begins to act as his pet, the collar around her neck being a mark of his dominance. But can the woman replace the beloved dog?

Of course, a film like this could never be made today, and indeed it would be bizarre to see such a sexist movie in the modern climate. But it works within its parameters, and the fact that Marcello and Catherine were real life lovers also helps, and in some ways makes it a more challenging piece too. Clearly they were a brave couple. The film looks splendid and is wonderfully shot by the reliable Ferreri, and the two leads lift what could have been a tiresome concept into something quite special. Marcello embodies the rustic painter and Deneuve is stunning as the new arrival in his life. Not Ferreri's best film, but certainly an interesting experiment and well worth a viewing for the chemistry between the two icons.

Deneuve herself later spoke about working with Ferreri and found him a confrontational personality.

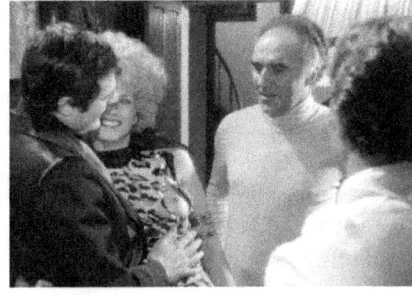

LA GRANDE BOUFFE (1973)

La Grande Bouffe, also known as The Big Feast and Blow-Out, was the most notorious and controversial film by Ferreri. It caused a sensation when it was screened at Cannes Film Festival in 1973, causing fist fights among the disagreeing crowd members, and even urging one to spit in the fact of Ferreri himself. This was a film so outrageous it was banned all together in Italy and was heavily censored and damned in most other countries. Famously, though more superficially, it was reported that Catherine Deneuve, who was still Marcello Mastroianni's lover at the time, refused to speak to him for a whole week after viewing it. Their affair continued of course, but no doubt seeing what Marcello got up to in this hedonistic, decadent, debauched film put a dint in the road of their future together.

The film itself concerns four old friends meeting up together to engage in a feast with the aim of eating themselves to death. We do not learn how these men met one another, but it's very clear there is much respect, love and admiration between the men. We are first introduced to Ugo (played by Ugo Tognazzi), a chef who has his own popular restaurant called The Biscuit Soup, the one who will prepare and present the culinary delights at the approaching festivities. Philippe (Philippe Noiret) is a magistrate whose mother died when he was two and still lives with his nanny, Nicole. Not only does he carry a framed picture of Nicole breastfeeding him when he was a babe in arms, but it is understood there is a strange sexual connection between the two. Clearly the man has mother issues, and Nicole is happy to use him to fulfil her own slightly warped erotic desires. The third friend is Marcello (played by Mastroianni), a pilot and serial womaniser who is led by his unquenchable thirst for the flesh of the female. The fourth man we are introduced to is Michel (Michel Piccoli), a TV producer who leaves the keys to his flat in the hands of his daughter, who he clearly knows is going to use it for parties.

The four arrive at a mansion belonging to Philippe, which was left to him by his father. It has a surrealistic garden with the atmosphere of a Giorgio De Chirico painting, and within its lavish exterior are countless works of art, exotic furnishings and a whole zoo of stuffed animals in glass cases. The fact the place is abandoned for the most part makes it even odder that upon arrival Philippe and his chums are greeted by the ancient caretaker Hector, who has with him a faithful hound named Catherine. He has prepared the cutlery for the feast, unaware of its sinister motive, and slowly leaves the boys to their fun.

The get together begins innocently enough with the friends over eating and even racing one another in the consumption of oysters. The aim is made clear; the men will eat themselves to death. But Marcello is unsure he can go so long without sex and that night ensures they are accompanied by three prostitutes. The atmosphere shifts up a gear and becomes more abandoned and hedonistic, though the intake of food is still the primary driving force of the meet-up. When a teacher arrives to show her pupils around the school, the film takes a strange turn. This seemingly wholesome woman named Andrea (Andrea Ferreol) arrives later to join in the festivities, but Philippe, believing her to be an innocent, is appalled she has arrived and is being forced to mix with the whores in this most sordid of scenarios. The eating and binging continues, and as Philippe and Andrea grow fond of each other, it is clear that Andrea is more liberated and debauched than the prostitutes. The first leaves in the morning, having vomited all night, while the other two leave later that day, leaving behind Andrea to be the strange enabler of the four men in their doomed one way mission to oblivion. As the four of them begin to drop off one by one, Andrea displays her endurance and loyalty to this most disturbing of causes.

The thing which troubles me most about La Grande Bouffe is the way that people tend to focus primarily on the excessive farting of the friends as their stomachs become bloated with the vast amounts of rich food. More attention seems to go on the literal overeating and indulgence than the clear symbolism behind such vulgar excess. Yes, Ferreri did state that the film should be taken as a literal story of four men overeating themselves to the grave, but there is a clear point or two being made here about the greed and careless abandon of the west. Capitalist society as we know it, built on a priggish hierarchal structure and driven by the pursuit of the so called finer things in life, is being torn to shreds throughout, mercilessly and wonderfully unsubtly I might add, by not only the mood in which the characters behave, but in the way the director makes the actors play it. Carelessly they down mouthfuls of elaborately prepared food, for which countless animals have had to give up their lives, guzzle drink and gorge on pudding until their bellies bloat. There are a few individual moments which stick out in the memory, both involving Michel; at one point he lavishly throws cake at a naked whore, calling a woman's body a vanity; secondly, when full to the point of near explosion, he lies there in a leotard being stuffed up with a huge heap of rich pâté. When one character at one point says in a pleading voice, I can't eat anymore, the feeder coldly suggests they imagine they are a starving boy in Bombay. Clearly, this is a statement on the unfairness of our society, the sickening greed of the rich, who have everything but know the true value of nothing. This is excess for excess's sake, and the men are joyously taking themselves to grave, as if to point out that it's all meaningless. Reduced to their basic human needs of eating, sleeping, shitting, farting and fucking, they soon cease to be men but bodies functioning, animalistic, primal beings slowly stuffing themselves into a stupor. This decadent, revolting decline into a greed that kills them may be symbolic, but it also makes for strange, demented entertainment too. Indeed, depending on your endurance, the film becomes a morbid treat, where each scene, every moment, every mouthful of rich food becomes a challenge to both the participant of the feast and the viewer at home.

Merely chronicling the feast says nothing about the movie itself. It is a wonderfully executed poem of excess, directed with assurance by Ferreri. Though a huge admirer of Luis Bunuel, Ferreri seemed to dislike people comparing his films to Bunuel's, even though Le Grande Bouffe is certainly Bunuelian, and in many ways even out does the Spanish master. Think of The Discreet Charm of the Bourgeoisie for example, Bunuel's satirical attack against the alleged upper society released a year before La Grande Bouffe, and one will see many similarities. Ferreri would have hated me comparing his film to the better known Bunuel classic, but there is much to compare, not only the tone of the film in its attitude, but also in its presentation, its straight faced surrealism and its aesthetic ghostliness. Still, they are very different beasts when it comes down to it, and La Grande Bouffe, though much less subtle, packs a greater punch and in the end is more enjoyable as a piece of cinema in itself.

The performances are excellent too. Though merely another member of the brilliant ensemble, Marcello's role is vital to the film and his characterisation is flawless. The other three, though happy to indulge, at least have some decency and know when to draw the line. Marcello though, sexually restless with a void within that is unfillable, is decadence embodied, with that look in his eye that says he would attempt to fuck anyone or anything that came his way. He is pumped up, arrogantly proclaiming that he cannot go a day without his orgasm, without fulfilling his needs as a man. But when he does engage in activities with the whore, it is empty, cold and ugly. When he screws the blonde hooker in the garage inside the antique car, it is beyond sleazy, and seems to only quench his thirst for a moment or two. Later, when he convinces Andrea to have sex with him, he fails to get an erection. Is it because she is purer in some way that he cannot bring himself to violate her, or perhaps because she has taken on the role of a kind of warped mother in the house? It's clear from how the men nuzzle into her bosom that there is a maternal quality they all relate to, and in some ways the group do devolve into a morbid kind of family unit; Ugo provides the food to fill their bellies, while Marcello is like the naughty, red blooded teenage son they can't reign in. It is after his inability to make love to Andrea that Marcello realises time is up for him. He abandons the eating and goes outside in the old car. While the others presume he has left for the night in the snow, he has in fact frozen to death at the driver's wheel. Michel is the most devastated, weeping uncontrollably while clinging to his friend, who is now stiff as a board and covered in particles of ice. Though they contemplate a burial, instead they carry his corpse to the kitchen, where it sits upright, just like one of the stuffed animals in the main hall.

The problem with La Grande Bouffe is not with the film itself, but with how people choose to view it. Like Peter Greenaway's The Cook, the Thief, His Wife and Her Lover, and also Pasolini's Salo, it's become a film to see for its excesses, a test of endurance, despite that all these films also carry an important message, where the excesses and more nauseating elements are applied to make points. Like the rape in Straw Dogs, the violence in A Clockwork Orange and the nude nuns in Ken Russell's The Devils (all, I might add, released in 1971), there is a subtext often overlooked, especially when viewed by younger people or fans of gross out genre cinema.

Today, La Grande Bouffe is not overtly shocking, but remains outrageous to say the least. Ferreri himself might be glad if he were around today that some of the grossest stuff in the picture might be overshadowed by the themes and satire beneath the excrement stained surface. Fans of Italian cinema and films for the mind may find their way to it and be pleasantly surprised that though it's a film liberated in its use of nudity, flatulence and sexism, it's making a good point, is visually stunning and features four brilliant performances from four icons of world cinema (not to mention Andrea's brilliant effort too). The problem is that fans of extreme cinema coming to it for titillation alone will be left disappointed, it not being an exploitative picture in any way. Indeed, it's repulsive, revolting and often sickening, but it is also a movie which remains relevant today, if not more now than when it was released. This is the greediest state the western world has been in, a time of selfish gratification without meaning or consideration for those with lesser opportunities. If anyone is uncomfortable with the way the four friends fill their bellies in La Grande Bouffe, it may be because they know they are as guilty in their own materialistic lives.

Though easily read as a parable of greed, there is also the theory that La Grande Bouffe perversely empowers the females. The prostitutes, damned quite often as beasts without morals, selling their flesh devoid of self respect, draw the line at the vile excesses of the men, four males we are definitely not supposed to admire or warm to in any way. Andrea may be the comforting mother figure, but she also becomes the most powerful person in the story, the men reduced to powerless boys in the face of her powerful femininity, holding the home together with quiet control. Meanwhile the boys are reduced to their most basic, animalistic needs.

At the time the film was highly controversial, which was reflected in contemporary reviews. Roger Ebert was not won over, writing "La Grande Bouffe, as nearly as I can tell, is essentially just a chronicle of gluttony and self-hate. La Grande Bouffe didn't leave me so much excited as exhausted. There is no doubt great significance in the way the characters talk about themselves, each other and French society; there is a double-reverse message to be found, I suppose, in the utter contempt with which the prostitutes in the movie are treated. The sight of bourgeois pigs being pigs is no doubt, from a certain point of view, an attack on their pigginess. Those would be the things the French intellectuals would argue about, but for me the film was more of an experience than a treatise; like The Exorcist, it doesn't have philosophical depth when you think about it, but in the theater it hammers your sensibilities. It's decadent, self-loathing, cynical and frequently obscene."

Only jazz singer and critic George Melly, well known for his love of Luis Bunuel, seemed to really get it. In the Observer he wrote "It is a serious rather than a titillating film. It's frequently physically nauseous, but never just nasty for its own sake, and the Greater London Film Council were quite right to reverse the BBFC's decision and allow us to see it uncut."

La Grande Bouffe won the prize from the critics at Cannes and has certainly endured a cult following. But the points it makes about society and capitalism will ultimately mean it gets brushed off by anyone unwilling to judge these materialistic, rather empty times we live in. If the message does get to you, that doesn't automatically mean you will want to endure over two hours of revolting excess, groping and gluttony. However, a dark sense of humour, a grasp of irony, a love of decent cinematography and anyone looking for liberated, expressionistic, untamed performances will no doubt be along for the ride. Marcello Mastroianni made a lot of good films in his career, but for me La Grande Bouffe is definitely one of the most memorable. It's fair to say that once you see it, you won't soon forget it.

DON'T TOUCH THE WHITE WOMAN (1974)

The final film Marcello Mastroianni made with Catherine Deneuve was Don't Touch the White Woman, a spoof western directed by Ferreri. Marcello stars as General Custer who is re-enacting a version of his Last Stand on a Paris building site, while European legends Michel Piccoli, Philippe Noiret and Ugo Tognazzi

star as other historical figures, resulting in the Battle of the Little Bighorn. The film is set in modern day Paris, but it blends itself with the old American west. Custer's arrival coincides with the business suits and powers that be deciding that he is the man for the job of ridding their city of the "scum" who bring it down.

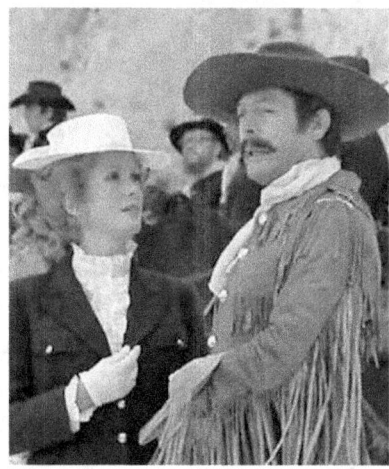

The four male leads worked wonders with Ferreri on their previous film together, the extraordinary La Grande Bouffe, but though Don't Touch the White Woman raises laughs and boasts great performances from the stars, it doesn't reach the same heights as their preceding masterpiece. It is however a sharp satire on American colonialism, and Ferreri, unflinching as ever, is not afraid to stick in the dagger. Engaging in its own way, it is far from Ferreri's best work. Yet there are some striking scenes which are hard to forget in their brutality. One scenario stays in the mind long after viewing; it features a taxidermist demonstrating how to stuff murdered Indians with newspaper, right in front of the Native children. Later on however, the man meets a bloody end during the battle, and in desperation tries to stuff himself with newspaper. There are other great scenes too, such as when Deneuve and Mastroianni can no longer control their sexual desires and she carries him to the bed, only after giving the cinema one of its most subtly erotic scenes, her face in close up, making near orgasmic noises of sexual excitement.

If Don't Touch the White Woman makes for mid boggling viewing for those who find it hard to enjoy such cinema, anyone who can see Ferreri's allegorical style for what it is will take much home from Don't Touch the White Woman. Possibly the most vicious attacks against America ever put to the screen, it remains worthy of your time.

THE LAST WOMAN (1976)

"The Last Woman," Ferreri said in 1977, "is a political film. All my films are… the relationship between men and the world they live in." The film, a harsh, jagged and often unpleasant one, highlights the unrest and confusion between the male and the female, with Depardieu, as in Ferreri's later Bye Bye Monkey, playing a kind of primal male who loves his kin but struggles to see eye to eye with the women in his life. He is an engineer, who after his wife leaves him, wishing to spread her feminist wings, takes on custody of his infant son and also begins an affair with his day care worker, Valerie, played by the gorgeous Ornella Muti. Their passionate and very physical relationship fulfils his animalistic side, but when the mother comes back into the picture, the tryst threatens his chances of retaining custody. As the film goes on, Depardieu becomes increasingly frustrated and torn. The finale, most unexpected even for Ferreri, is one of the most outrageous final reels in film history.

This is a real stand out from Gerard's early years as a world renowned star, once again showing himself to be the bravest, most daring and least squeamish actor of his time. Still harbouring those street smarts, he is the raw male, symbolising the masculine caveman, quite often standing nude with chest stuck out, protecting the child he holds in one arm and holding his woman in the other, who he takes with passion whenever he pleases. This is the kind of Ferreri film they threw sexist and misogynist claims at, and though one can understand why it may be viewed negatively as pure sexism, Ferreri is merely reflecting a certain dissatisfaction amongst the more forceful, non-progressive, traditionalist males of the world. But for Ferreri, such claims were part of his job, and he expected a backlash seeing as he was exploring taboo ideas. He was damned a complete sexist when he made La Grande Bouffe, especially when he presented the four friends treating the hired women like the meat they gorged on in their orgy of decadence, but those critics were missing the point. As in Bye Bye Monkey, another Depardieu/Ferreri gem, he laments the downfall of the male and the uprising of the new modern woman. He is not saying this shift is right or wrong, he is simply commentating on it, another "political" film about the conflicts so inevitable between the opposing sexes.

Gerard is magnificent in this Cesar nominated effort, a man-child who will touch, fondle, feel and devour whatever he feels like. It is a primal, vital and quite often frighteningly intense performance, Depardieu the animal man turned up to eleven. In one sequence, unashamedly naked, he tries to attack a woman with a phallic object, a gigantic penis in fact, a moment which symbolises his anger and frustrations, that he merely wants to fuck and own, and fails to see where he fits into the feminist era.

The film was deemed too controversial for modern tastes and was banned in various countries. Even to this day, it's hard work tracking it down and it remains elusive, which is particularly frustrating for Ferreri completists and fans of Depardieu at his best. Thankfully though, finding The Last Woman is not impossible, but a bit of detective work might be in order. Easily offended viewers will, perhaps understandably, be put off by certain imagery in the film and Ferreri's cynical, often crude and occasionally heartless approach, but some valid and thought provoking themes are explored. The baby himself could be seen as a symbol for Depardieu's own sulky childishness, rather like the ape in Bye Bye Monkey symbolised his primal urges.

The Last Woman is often a challenge, most certainly isn't for everyone, and occasionally leaves a bad taste in the mouth. But it is a very important Ferreri work, in a line of films which included Liza, La Grande Bouffe, Don't Touch the White Woman and Bye Bye Monkey. Though veering off now and then, and sometimes questionable with its upfront imagery, this unflinching film is essential Depardieu and a prime example of why he flew so quickly to world fame in the mid to late 1970s.

BYE BYE MONKEY (1978)

Marco Ferreri repeatedly pushed the boundaries in his films, but Bye Bye Monkey is among his most extreme, unsettling, thought provoking, and rewarding movies - and that is saying something. Though perhaps less focused and powerful than La Grande Bouffe (in my view his true masterpiece), Bye Bye Monkey is certainly wilder (if that were possible), weirder, and seems to be saying so much more about society as a whole, but especially modern America. It is also, of course, brilliant.

Gerard Depardieu stars as Lafayette, a New York based electrician who does work for a wax museum run by the very strange Andreas (James Coco), mostly focused on Ancient Imperial Rome, and a feminist theatre troupe who need him for their lighting tricks. There are other key figures in the film too; for instance, Marcello Mastroianni plays Luigi, an extremely eccentric immigrant who hangs around with other unusual characters near the beach, including Mrs Toland, played by Geraldine Fitzgerald. One day, the theatre troupe, who are playing with the idea of exploring rape in their dramatic work, realise they have no experience of it themselves, so decide to rape Lafayette One girl, Angelica (Abigal Clayton), acts as the chief rapist and afterwards begins to date him.

But things haven't even got started at this point. One day, Lafayaette, Luigi and other friends take a visit to the beach, where they find a gigantic sculpture of an ape (most literally a deceased King Kong; symbolically the bulky remains of manhood), lying in a heap on the sand. This image is striking enough of course, but to make it even more remarkable is the fact that an actual baby chimp emerges from its folds. Luigi picks it up, insisting it's his son, but the baby falls into the care of Lafayette when Luigi claims he's too old to be a dad. The chimp moves into Lafayette's run down, seedy apartment, which is infested with rats. As the movie goes on, Lafayette and the chimp bond, having various adventures together as they make their way around the more run down parts of New York City. The atmosphere is unnerving for much of the film, but strangely there is true warmth between man and ape. However, in the final quarter or so, the movie becomes increasingly dark, unflinchingly so, and ends in the kind of tragedy the whole film seems to have been silently building towards, in what is one of the saddest and most horrifying climaxes to any picture I have ever seen.

Though Ferreri often stated in interviews that everything in his films should be enjoyed at face value, taken literally and not dissected for hidden meanings until all the fun was ruined, there is no doubting that he was being mischievous with such a statement, for his films are full of symbolism. The symbolism in La Grande Bouffe for instance was blatantly obvious and more effective than subtly applied allegories could ever be. In Bye Bye Monkey, with the narrative being anarchic, and with nothing out of reach of Ferreri's savage satire, it's harder to pin point what he precisely means in each scene.

Some have seen Bye Bye Monkey as an anti feminist film - even an anti female film! After all, Lafayette chooses the ape over his girlfriend who is carrying his child, though in my view his bond with the ape merely reflects Lafayette's primal humanity, him being a man living in a world of crumbling values drawn to the simplicity and purity of the creature. Indeed, clinging to the chimp ensures Lafayette soaks in some of that innocence. Even though one cannot deny that Ferreri paints the feminist troupe as dangerously angry and aggressive, they are in fact the only stable people in the whole film. For me, the feminist theories are misleading; clearly, with Ferreri depicting New York as some crumbling hellhole, the film laments the lack of humanity in modern society, with the ape as child, wide eyed and innocent in the face of corruption and decay. But one could validly say that this film, and some of his others, also laments the death of traditional manhood, pointing out his view that man himself was being robbed off his masculinity out of guilt and shame. (Mastroiani's Luigi seems to sum this up in one line, when sexually frustrated shouting out, "I have some kind of monster between my legs!") Though this arguably misogynistic view will automatically put off some viewers, it's best to keep an open mind. Again, it is not as simple as Ferreri mourning the future of masculinity or indeed mankind itself, but perhaps the values of old. And just because his characters are tearful of the changing times, does not mean Ferreri or the younger characters are. This in mind, there is so much haunting and disturbing imagery here that it's impossible to rip it of its vitality by trying to hang meanings on every frame. It's best in some ways to sit back and enjoy (or depending on your view, endure) the odd ball delights unfolding before your eyes.

Depardieu is brilliant in the lead role, but Mastroianni's Luigi is in some ways the most engaging, mysterious and bizarre character in the film. An ageing Italian, he paints the figurines in the museum, solemnly I might add, always complaining that he cannot find love or sex in America because modern women don't respect their elders, or the old fashioned way a man once related to a woman. Marcello would play a man stuck in feminist hell two years later in Fellini's masterpiece City of Women, but here he is so wildly eccentric, so utterly mad in fact, that he seems beyond being able to comprehend modern life on any level, least of all the modern female. Fellini made his points on feminism clear, while Ferreri hides them under the scenarios. Ferreri's intentions aside, for me, Luigi is one of Mastroianni's most interesting and watchable creations. In the documentary I Remember, Marcello recalled how fun it was to make Bye Bye Monkey, in that they were free to make things up as they went along. And it's clear that Marcello was liberated in his role, letting his imagination and creativity run wild. Always moist eyed, often with tears running down his cheeks, he is a raw man in torment; defeated, lost, always a "wop", an outsider, someone on the fringes, not just within society, but even amongst his fellow eccentrics. In one scene he does look briefly happy, when he begins an impromptu tap dance with his cane. When he drops it however, he instantly resumes his sombre stance.

Unfortunately he meets a tragic and extremely disturbing end, but it's also one of his most memorable exits.

Bye Bye Monkey won the main prize at Cannes, even though some critics were hopelessly lost amidst its surrealistic liberation. That

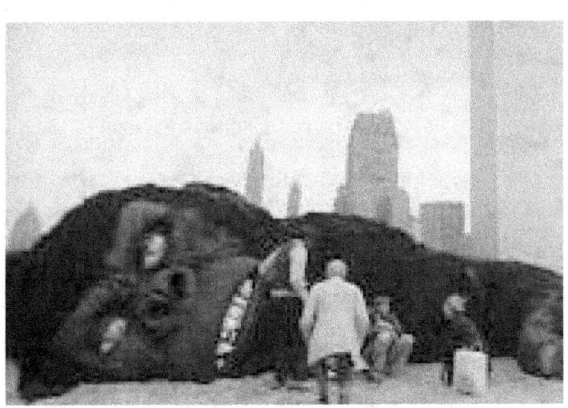

such an avant garde film could win a major prize is indeed a sign that cinema has gone down hill. Put this on for a young fan of superhero flicks or Star Wars space operas and they'd be bored, or worst of all offended after a few scenes. For those with an attention span longer than five minutes however, Bye Bye Monkey is a thought provoking, funny, often very bleak but ultimately enjoyable (if that is indeed the correct word) and hugely rewarding film of imagination, a movie with more ideas in five of its minutes than any modern blockbuster has in all its CGI stuffed scenes of nothingness. Its streets devoid of life, save the scurrying of

rats and the odd eccentric, stick in the mind forever, reminding this viewer of Giorgio De Chirico's early paintings, empty streets inhabited only by shadows of figures just out of shot. Love it or hate it, you will never see another movie like Bye Bye Monkey.

YERMA (1978)

Ferreri's last film of his golden period of the 1970s was a TV adaptation of Federico Garcia Lorca's Yerma, a very obscure oddity today which thankfully to the joys of the internet is easier to find than you might imagine - if you are willing to do some detective work that is.

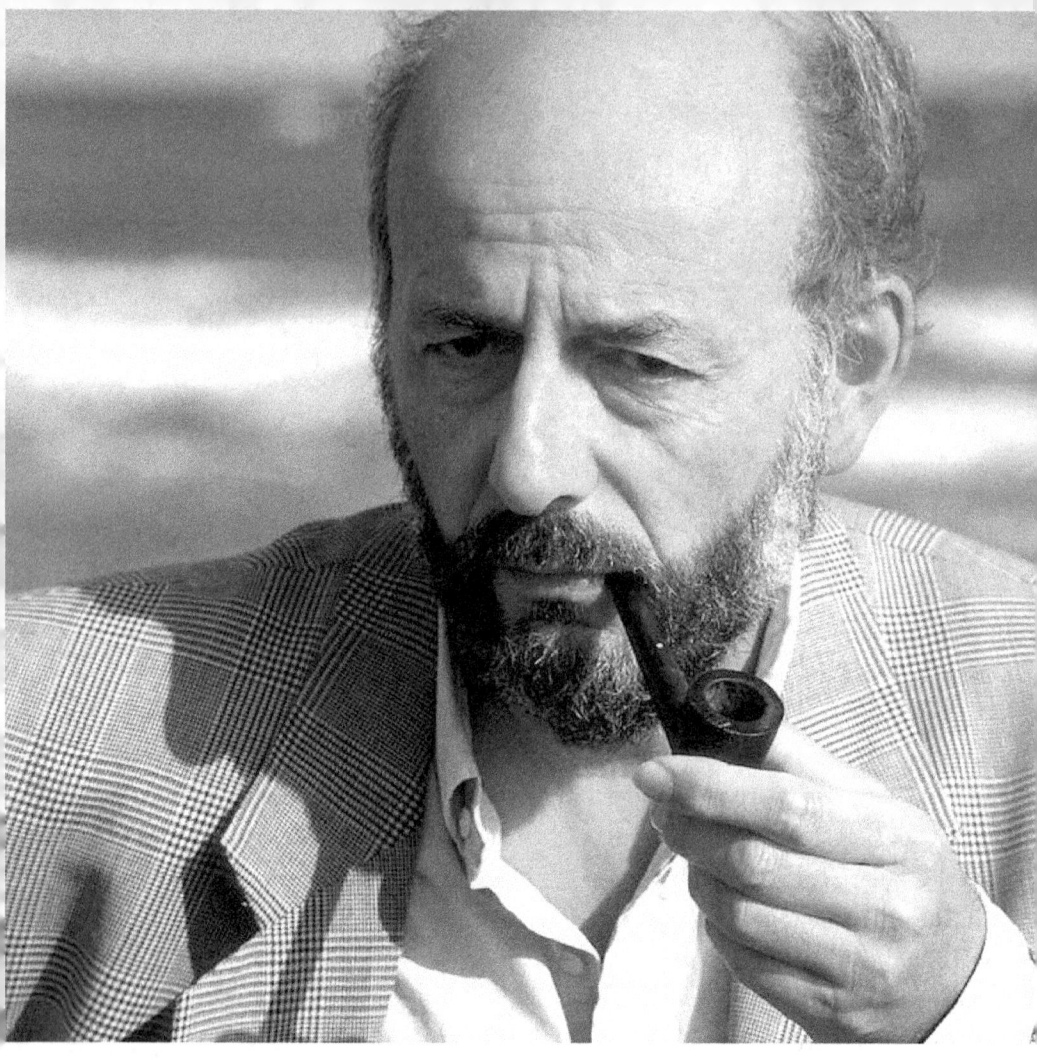

THE BEST OF BERTRAND BLIER

Bertrand Blier is one of the most influential European directors of the past fifty years. Since the 1970s he has made some of the most anarchic and controversial movies in France, often starring the great Gerard Depardieu. Here is my run down of the finest films Blier has directed...

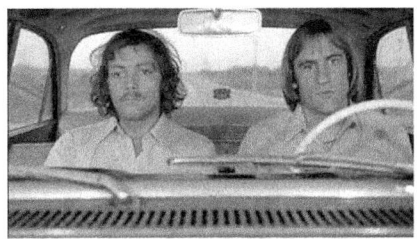

GOING PLACES (1974)

The film which signalled the true arrival on our screens of Gerard Depardieu was Bertrand Blier's outrageous black comedy, Going Places, titled Les Valseuses in French and based on Blier's own novel. Here, the twenty five year old actor, still fresh faced and dangerous, starred as Jean-Claude, who with his friend Pierrot (Patrick Dewaere) embarks on a road trip around France. The two young men are petty criminals and spend their time hustling, stealing, taking what they want and engaging in the most sordid of activities.

Going Places begins with the terrible duo stealing the car of a hairdresser, who pulls a gun on them when they return his vehicle (their defence is that they merely borrowed his car and always intended to bring it back). When they snatch the weapon, they take his assistant Marie-Ange (Miou-Miou) as a prisoner. While acting as her captors, they both have sex with her, but grow frustrated with the fact she cannot achieve an orgasm. Quickly dumping her off, they grow tired of frigid young ladies (lumps of meat as Jean-Claude refers to them) and opt to find a more mature woman who will be in control of her body, but also grateful for the attention of two young men.

They wait outside a prison, where Jeanne (the wonderful Jeanne Moreau) is just being released. Following her down the road, they latch on to her and quiz her about her life. Learning she has no money and nowhere to go, the boys hand over some of their stolen cash and wait outside a department store while Jeanne buys some new clothes. They take her to a cafe and enjoy a lavish meal, before deciding to get a hotel room and have a threesome. The next morning, while the young men sleep, Jeanne goes into the spare bedroom in the hotel, takes out the gun, and shoots herself, not in the head, but up her own vagina. Horrified, the boys get dressed and rush out of the hotel through the basement.

Researching the letters in the dead woman's case, they learn of her imprisoned son and the fact he too is about to be released. Picking him up, they take Jacques to their country retreat, where Marie-Ange is now set up as their female accomplice/casual sex partner. There is a new obsession with ensuring she achieves a climax, which Jacques, not Jean-Claude or Pierrot, manages to help her reach. While they toy with the idea of being a crime committing foursome, this plan crumbles apart. The final ten minutes involve the two boys and Marie-Ange coming across a family enjoying a picnic by a river, and plucking the daughter (played by a young Isabelle Huppert) away from the family unit in order to ceremoniously de-flower her. The film ends with the trio, after dropping off the young girl having

taken her virginity, driving off in their latest stolen car, entering a long dark tunnel, going places but really heading nowhere.

Blier's film is a wonderful black comedy, raising genuine laughs which are inevitably tinged with guilt once you realise what you are actually laughing at. Both uncomfortably confrontational and genuinely hilarious, Blier succeeds because one is not asked to judge or celebrate the young men's shenanigans. Yes what they are doing is wrong, but the film is not weighed down by judgements, nor encumbered by a conscience. We follow the men in their aimless journey, not because we like them (indeed, they are two of the most loathsome louts ever shown on screen), but because we are desperate to know what's coming next. Their adventures do not seem contrived and the humour is never forced; it's very natural indeed, and played with the kind of genuine straight forwardness which makes it truly funny rather than merely amusing in a broad, caricature-like sense.

Blier's direction is assured and unfussy, while his script (co-written with Philippe Cumarcay) is often genuinely shocking and to some will be offensively misogynistic. That said, Pierrot and Jean-Claude are not gentlemen, and their harsh, often grotesque way with words fits the story perfectly. Yet had the film not starred Depardieu and Dewaere as the two restless crooks, Going Places may have been unwatchable. Depardieu in particular is brilliant, looking like he has genuinely just walked from the streets where he might have been swindling some poor unsuspecting person. Had we been told he had just stolen a car to drive to the shooting location, we would not have been surprised. No performance this good could possibly have gone unnoticed and it's perfectly logical that he became an overnight star after the film's smash success in France (it was the third most successful film that year). Alive, often frightening and seemingly always on the cusp of doing something either disgusting or totally unexpected, Depardieu's Jean-Claude is one of his finest cinematic creations. It seems though that the danger so evident in the performance was not entirely brought out of thin air. According to reports, Depardieu was still very much the wild man of his youth while making Going Places. Blier recalled that they often had to keep checking on him, as he had a habit of going off into the rougher areas of where they were shooting to pick fights in bars.

Going Places caused quite a stir upon release, being both commercially successful and extremely controversial, due to the dialogue, the lurid content, casual, blatant sex scenes and general carelessness of the characters. It was hedonism at his wildest, and seems to have divided audiences and critics alike. Roger Ebert, though seeing some worth in it, seems to have been sickened overall: "Despite its occasional charm, its several amusing moments and the touching

79

scenes played by Jeanne Moreau, Going Places is a film of truly cynical decadence. It's also, not incidentally, the most misogynistic movie I can remember; its hatred of women is palpable and embarrassing. I came away from Going Places feeling that I'd spent two hours in the company of a filmmaker I would never want to meet."

Such critics seemed to miss the point. Blier himself was not the sexist one, he was just a man presenting certain views held by a particular type of young male. The fact he made us laugh and gasp at such men though, is an achievement indeed, and it's this mix of reactions which makes Going Places truly unique. Blier went on to further success in his career as a filmmaker, winning an Oscar for his 1977 classic Get Your Handkerchiefs Out (again, with Gerard Depardieu), making seminal films like Buffet Froid and Merci La Vie, not to mention the Cesar and Cannes Special Prize winning Too Beautiful For You, but there is a vitality, energy and genuine danger in Going Places that makes it, quite possibly, his most lasting and enthralling work.

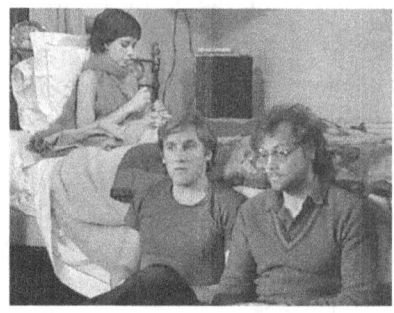

GET OUT YOUR HANDKERCHIEFS (1978)

Bertrand Blier is one of the most unique and individual directors in cinema history. Truly surrealistic, his films dispense with all logic, but rather than dissolving in a form of Dada nonsense, they give birth to their own new logic in the process, presenting the viewer with so many unexpected, provocative twists and turns that after a while, thanks largely to the deadpan reactions of the actors, the viewer accepts them at face value. After ten minutes of any Blier film, nothing can be questioned;

80

nor, for that matter, can it be answered.

Depardieu had become a star in Blier's wonderfully mad Going Places, and his next film with the director, some four years later with Gerard established firmly as a new bright light of world cinema, was the outrageously funny, and often plain shocking, Get Out Your Handkerchiefs.

Undeniably subversive, it seems bizarre today that such a straight laced institution as the Oscars would give such a grimy, strange film its Best Foreign Language Film gong - which it did, in 1978. It's hard to imagine it doing so in today's social climate.

The film stars Depardieu as Raoul, a young driving instructor married to Solange (Carole Laure), and experiencing a certain dissatisfaction with their stale, increasingly strained relationship. Dining out one Sunday lunch time, Raoul becomes overwhelmed with frustration, and insists that his wife is sick of his face, and that she needs, in his words, "a new pair of eyes and balls". Driven to cheer up his wife, he goes to another table and meets Stephane (Patrick Dewaere), a teacher reading about Mozart, and offers him the opportunity to finish the meal with his wife and hopefully make her smile. As the film progresses, the three characters become a trio, each man taking it in turns to spend the night with Solange in a bid to liven her up. When both men come to the bizarre conclusion that Solange's passionless state (she never smiles or laughs, preferring to sit quietly knitting for hours on end) will be lifted by a pregnancy, they attempt to impregnate her. The neighbour also enters the situation, though he does not engage with Solange and merely joins in with the boys and their weird obsession with the life and work of Mozart, who they regularly lament.

The film takes a weird twist when Stephane takes a class of boys to a summer camp, and Solange and Raoul accompany him as unlikely assistant teachers. Unexpectedly, Solange falls for Christian (Riton

Liebman), a 13 year old child genius who enchants her from the word go. Bullied by the other children, she takes pity on him, invites him into her bed and eventually, after a brief disagreement, opens him up to the wonders of femininity. When he expresses his reluctance to return to his family, he is sent to the boarding school, but the terrible trio kidnap him, as Solange can not go on living without her boy. As Raoul and Stephane become more jealous of the young boy, there comes forth a revelation which, even to the usual standards of Blier's work, is most unexpected, though not at all illogical given the way things have been heading. It is perhaps one of the best finales in the history of European cinema.

"I thought about the film on and off for about three years before I began writing," Blier said in 1979. "So when I did write, the ideas came out spontaneously. I almost didn't know what I was writing. What I like in films and in literature are stories and characters that surprise me."

Get Out Your Handkerchiefs certainly gives its viewer a lot to think about, but most of all it offers us much to react to, and after each viewing one is forced (or feels the need) to sit back and re-think what we've seen and experienced. Totally individualistic, it manages to tear everything out of the rule book, reshuffle it, batter it beyond recognition and then put it all back together into a mutated but totally real new form. The structure, as it is, is down to Blier's skill at thinking outside the box. Blier says he wrote the script from the middle onwards, beginning with a fantasising scenario on Mozart, and even contemplating the idea of having an actor portray Mozart during the scenes where Raoul and Stephane muse and dream of the great composer. Though this was abandoned, Mozart's music was to become an essential part of the film, blending seamlessly with Georges Delerue's Cesar Award winning score.

"The idea came to me to make a film about two imbeciles who speak about Mozart as they would about soccer," Blier recalled. "I wrote the scene very quickly, and it appears just as I wrote it then in the film."

Blier had Depardieu and Dewaere in mind for these two afore mentioned imbeciles from the start, having already won great acclaim with them as the two leads in 1974's Going Places. Again, the pair work wonderfully together, at first having conflicts but by the midway point becoming close, if not like brothers, and as in Going Places when it gets going, even dressing in matching clothes. Dewaere embodies the nervy and obsessive intellectual with ease, a mile away from the nasty brute he portrayed in Going Places. It's one of the finest performances from his all too brief film career (he committed suicide in 1982 at the age of 35). Depardieu, again, is marvellous here, playing a curious blend of cuckold and chauvinist, a man who will do anything to "please" his wife but also insist that he knows best when it comes to her happiness. Essentially loaning her to another man, he is a misogynist through and through, another rough and ready male who, though becoming more sophisticated as he begins to appreciate Mozart, seems to degenerate into an even more primitive being as he sees his wife fall for the purer boy he is bitterly jealous of. In a very difficult role, Carole Laure excels, perfecting the bored female put-upon by two old fashioned men, craving a man (in this case, boy) who will let her be who she is. The film may have been accused of being sexist (in the US the Village Voice called it "extraordinarily misogynous by any standards"), but it is more a study of sexism, with Laure's character ultimately getting one up on both Raoul and Stephane in the end.

Rather unexpectedly, it was a smash in America, no doubt because of its Oscar win. When it screened at the New York Film Festival, it was both booed and applauded. Critics either loved it or seemed to find it too bizarre and curious. Pauline Kael, the high priestess of American film criticism, said it made her "unreasonably happy", while Time Out claimed it to be "erratic and often hilarious. Somewhere in all this chaos, the movie firmly puts the boot into mainstream French comedy, substituting absurd and amiable bad taste for the intellectual rigor mortis of which Parisians are so proud." Though they had a point, and indeed Blier's film is a savage beating of the clichéd French comedy, it also exists on its own merit as an engaging, anarchic story which does away with all conventions and creates a sub genre of its own. As good as Depardieu and the others in the cast are, one can't help but feel it is Blier's show entirely.

In an interview with the Washington Post in 1979, Blier said "In France people don't laugh very much at it. For example, when a 13-year-old child gets a 25-year-old woman pregnant, for me that's funny. But in France, they say, No, that's impossible. Invariably, you shock some people and stimulate others. When everyone agrees, that's a very bad sign. As a filmmaker, it's best to stretch yourself to your limits. Handkerchiefs' is my favourite of my films so far, and in appearance, yes, it is more whimsical and less abrasive, less political than Going Places. Yet, really I think Handkerchiefs is the more subversive film. In Going Places, where the two men steal cars and hold up picnickers and force women to submit to them, the provocation is visible. Handkerchiefs, on the other hand, is a very soft, very seductive film. But, if you look carefully, all the traditional values are upset here: the couples, the family, maternity."

Though eager to follow his inspiration and go against clichés, he also noted that the film had no message. "I detest messages, false messages perhaps; I like to play with false messages." He did however feel that he was a man qualified to explore women's problems, given he was never a macho singleton and when making the film was married with a child. He did however add that a man should never deny his masculinity. The key to Blier's views on men and women is balance; he clearly thought the exaggerated and hysterical aspects of feminism were absurd, and that extreme machismo was totally out of order. "The men in Handkerchiefs aren't exactly idiots," Blier commented, "but they come pretty close to that. They're very intelligent in their hearts, but more fragile than the woman in their heads. In their own petty way, these two men try to revolutionize things, and the result is catastrophic."

In redefining the French farce, Blier highlights the shortcoming of both sexes, but punctuates his musings with pure surrealism, the idea that everything which happens, no matter how seemingly out of the ordinary, should be accepted as mundane. Fans of Depardieu will be delighted, as it is certainly one of the strongest efforts from his whole varied and rich filmography, as well as one of the finest films he has ever been a part of.

A 2019 retrospective review in the LA Times summed it up thus: "And yet the movie's style is pure deadpan — bored, even, at times, which in a way creates its own blackly humorous fizz regarding our taste for exhaustive sexual escapades, endless psychologizing and the timeless (tired?) allure of the unfathomable object of desire. (Were the signposts of the French New Wave Blier's eye-poking target?) Get Out Your Handkerchiefs may not shock the way it once did, but it remains the purest expression of Blier's comic métier, treating naughty ideas with the straightest of faces."

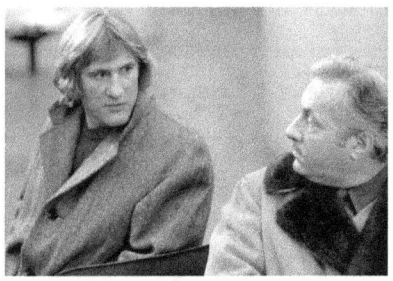

BUFFET FROID (1979)

The teaming of Bertrand Blier and Gerard Depardieu, in its many varied forms, has always produced films of an extraordinary and unique quality.

They first worked together on 1974's Going Places, before earning more world wide notice for Get Your Handkerchiefs Out in 1977. Buffet Froid, released in 1979, is often seen as their finest collaboration and is sometimes ranked as one of the greatest French films of all time (Time Out for instance, placed it in their top 50). A jagged, unpredictable and fearlessly surrealistic experience, Buffet Froid is a film like no other and one can honestly say that there is nothing to which you can compare it, not even other Blier works. Considering the success he had enjoyed before its release, makes it something of a surprise that Blier's Buffet Froid was so misunderstood upon release and enjoyed only a modest amount of success. What is not surprising however, is how it's built up such a healthy cult following in the past couple of decades.

Depardieu is at his most paradoxically appealing and anonymous as Tram, an unemployed no-hoper whose life begins to change beyond all recognition one night when he chances upon a man in the subway. Sitting beside him, with no one else around, he presents the man the knife he conceals on his person and asks him to take it, before he does something silly with it. Irritated, the man reluctantly takes the blade and places it on a seat beside him. When the two men look round however, the knife has vanished into thin air. After the stranger leaves on a train arriving at that pivotal moment, Depardieu's hopeless Tram walks off aimlessly. Later in the night he passes the man in a tunnel, and sticking bloodly out of his belly as he lays against the wall is Tram's own blade. Confused, Tram heads home to the apartment block where only he and his wife live, and upon his return tries to tell her about the murder in the subway while eating his late night dinner. Informed by his wife that a man has moved into the flat above them, Tram pays him a late night visit. Learning he is a chief inspector, Tram becomes animated and tells Insp. Morvandiau (played by Bernard Blier) of the murder, but the cop wants nothing to do with it, telling him to go home and that he is spoiling his relaxing evening. From here on, the film goes from one irrational twist to another, with all logic and reason non existent as Tram's odyssey becomes wilder and wilder. The other characters include a creepy lady-killer (played by Jean Carmet) who adds Tram's wife to his list of murders, and then, along with the cop and a widow of a man Tram himself ends up slaying (named Genevieve, played by Genevieve Page), becomes an active member of this unlikely gang who find themselves stumbling through an increasingly bizarre chain of events.

Blier's film is an undeniable out and out comedy. Though occasionally shocking, he resists explicit imagery or language this time, avoiding the confrontational outrage of Going Places and instead succeeding in bringing a Surrealist masterpiece painting to life before our eyes. As with Blier's best work, a point is being made beneath the stylised surface; the city is an animal, an unforgiving beast which conjures nightmares and turns all humans into amoral, soulless beings, confused by their lives and unable to make sense of those they come into contact with. The buildings are ugly, angular, threatening, and the neighbourhoods are bleak, unfriendly, the kind of places you would avoid if you had any sense. Indeed, Blier's city is a relentless, unforgiving place, a scrap yard of urban decay and human bewilderment.

Blier blends styles and themes to create a masterwork of his own, no doubt influenced by the great Luis Bunuel (especially in the matter-of-fact presentation of the Surrealism, all played out with straight faces and without cartoonish exaggerations), but also conjuring up a paranoiac mood that could easily and fairly be described as Kafka-esque. Though there is no trial, one thinks of Kafka's masterpiece due to the relentlessness and cold distance between the characters and their harsh environments. As with true

Surrealism, as its creator and "pope" Andre Breton insisted upon, the characters do not react to the absurdities of their situation, but treat them as ordinary and expected.

Despite the film's detours into the truly bizarre and quite often the macabre, Buffet Froid remains uproariously good fun. This is thanks not only to Blier's script, but also the wonderful performances. Bernard Blier is unsettlingly good as the Inspector, a man who represents the law but bends it to his liking and reacts in the opposite manner to what one might expect when he chances upon, or is presented with a crime. Carmet is very convincing as the sneaky killer, a man who cannot resist killing if he happens to be alone with a woman. Though clearly demented, he seems to be the only one who knows just how alienating and dangerous a place the city is, and is also the only man who knows how to express his disenchantment with the urban experience.

Depardieu is our eyes and ears through this increasingly contorted but strangely more and more acceptable trip into the unknown. This is another one of his lay about lost souls, in the same line as the small time thug of Loulou, the curious motorcyclist of Maitresse and the fiendish crook of Going Places. He perfectly nails the mood, a man at first puzzled by the turn of events but increasingly accepting of it, expectant even by each new revelation waiting around the corner. It's worth noting of course that the one event which kick starts this descent into non-logic is not even recalled by the perpetrator, namely the murder of the stranger in the subway by the blade of Tram. Only at the end, when he is forced to face up to what he has done, does he acknowledge the event as his own doing. The performance is a tour de force because Depardieu makes it all look so natural, never reacting to the scenarios he is faced with. A lesser actor could not have pulled it off with such style.

Critics at the time, especially in America, were lost in the madness.

The New York Times, clearly puzzled, wrote "Buffet Froid is well titled. It's a meal composed entirely of side-dishes. There's no main course, and when the meal is over, you're still waiting for something serious to eat. The movie is a collection of random sketches in the service of no dominant idea."

Despite such write-ups, Blier's film is now a classic. Time Out, writing of the film in 2012, declared it a "rigorously absurd contemporary film noir," adding that though it introduced every trademark of the genre, it resisted providing the explanations or motivations of them.

TROP BELLE POUR TOI
(1989)

Gerard Depardieu was back with Bertrand Blier once more with Trop Belle Pour Toi, known in English as Too Beautiful For You. Closer to the work of Jean Luc Godard than their previous work together, Too Beautiful For You constantly plays with logic, ones idea of what makes sense and what doesn't. This provocative, confrontational and darkly funny film more than measures up to the likes of Going Places, Buffet Froud and Get Out Your Handkerchiefs, even if there is a shift in style.

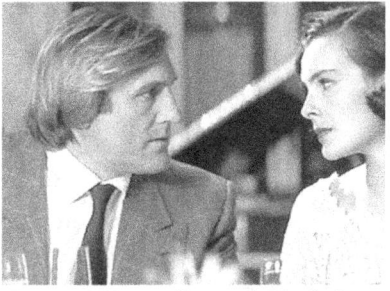

It stars Depardieu as Barthelemy Bernard, a BMW dealership owner who seems to have it all; good job, plenty of money, status, lots of friends, a child, a beautiful home and an equally beautiful wife, played by the striking Carole Bouquet. Tipping everything upside down early on in the film, Gerard's character falls for Colette (Josiane Balasko), a plain and seemingly ordinary secretary he has recently hired. She does not have the beauty of his wife, but then she doesn't have her shortcomings either,

her delusions and pretences. As their affair continues, Barthelemy sees his life change beyond recognition; all the while the music of Schubert plays loudly, not always in the background, but often interfering with and even dominating whole scenes.

Too Beautiful For You is not an instantly "easy" film to watch, but then if you are up for a challenge it is worth sticking with and getting used to. In fact, its unconventional qualities end up enriching it, lifting it from more straight forward and predictable romantic dramas. While this kind of tale would normally involve a middle aged man cheating on his dour wife with a beauty, immediately Blier decides to invert expectations and lampoon the popular cliché, indeed as he had in Buffet Froid and Get Out Your Handkerchiefs. Rich in visuals and ideas, it is also ironic, self aware (in a good way) and mischievous, being full of typical Blier humour. It also shares something with Get Out Your Handkerchiefs; an obsession with music from a single composer, with

the earlier Mozart here being replaced by the more intrusive and often irritating Schubert. While characters are forced to shout over the music in certain scenes where someone is playing Schubert a little too loudly, Depardieu himself is driven to near insanity by it, to the point that at the very end he shouts to the camera how much Schubert has been winding him up for the previous 90 minutes. He breaks down the fourth wall, merely to align himself with our own belief that movie soundtracks can manipulate and often ruin the direction of a film. Paradoxically, by highlighting this flaw in popular movies, Blier creates something unique, where his main character has become aware of the soundtrack.

Blier's film is not merely a repeat of themes and concepts from earlier work, but a totally fresh and individual film in its own right. Characters speak to camera, openly express frustration and thoughts usually limited to the inner mind, and in other scenes they appear in flashback within the new scene, so that past and present overlap and cohabitant time. Rather than setting up a straight forward narrative, Blier establishes his unique approach to this meditation on love and relationships, not to mention the enigma of desire itself, with striking images which highlight Depardieu's new found passion in contrast to what he has at home. As beautiful as his wife may be, he is also bored by her confidence, her self assuredness and control over those around her. One scene early on is key; it involves the couple having dinner with friends, she holding court with a pretentious monologue which, though enrapturing the others, leaves Depardieu cold. "Is there a point to this?" he asks. Right away, he is refreshed by the plain secretary's openness, her straight forward air and the other qualities which the more beautiful naturally do not possess. This is a film of infatuation, about the mystery of attraction. Right away, we wonder what Depardieu sees in her which he doesn't have at home. Half way through we understand it more, but at the end we are just as confused and conflicted as he is.

Blier's film was very acclaimed upon release. It also swept the Cesar Awards, winning Best Film, Best Writing, Best Directing, Best Editing and Best Director for Carole Bouquet, as well as the Special Prize at Cannes Film Festival. Elsewhere the film was held up as a masterpiece. John Mount wrote of the film for Empire: "Bertrand Blier, who has always tried to provide something to offend everyone in his surreal, black comedies, delivers his finest outing in years in this parable on the dangers of confusing your stereotypes and taking a mistress as a wife and vice versa. Depardieu has a field day as the wandering husband, torn between two women for all the wrong reasons and crumbling into indecision with cruel, ironic results. All very French, of course, and although the mordant humour and various outrageous twists look in danger of unravelling at the end, Depardieu's indiscretion finally comes home to roost with a satisfying vengeance. Social observation with a sledgehammer."

Roger Ebert, though admitting it was a challenge, was impressed with Blier's commitment, writing "This is grown up love, not the silly adolescent posturing of Hollywood sex symbols. It is love beyond sex, beyond attraction, beyond lust. It is the love of need..." On Depardieu, firstly describing him as a man who looks scared that he is always about to break something, he wrote, "(he) is one of the most endlessly fascinating actors of our time. He works constantly, in roles of such variety that to list them is astonishing. Here he plays an ordinary man, one of the most difficult roles in the movies. He makes his passion believable because he never over acts it."

Indeed, this is a tricky role for him, but Depardieu pulls it off wonderfully, never over cooks the part, nor makes anything seem unbelievable in this purely surreal film, one which no doubt Breton himself would have approved of. He is natural in a film that is anything but, and that in itself makes this performance a tour de force and among his finest portrayals of the everyman faced with a challenging predicament.

Too Beautiful For You is perhaps the finest study of that phenomenon known as amour fou, and is certainly among Blier's most satisfying films.

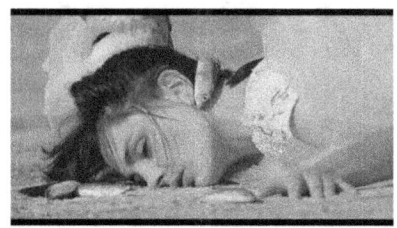

MERCI LA VIE (1991)

To claim one film by Bertrand Blier is more subversive, anarchic or funnier than any other may seem like doing the visionary himself a disservice (after all, all his films are brilliant), but though Merci La Vie is often seen as a minor entry in his filmography, to some a less focused, less satisfactory experience than his more celebrated work, in some ways it's his most liberated and therefore most liberating work. As it begins we assume - misguidedly maybe - that the film may follow a more or less cohesive narrative. Ten minutes in though, and one realises Merci La Vie is not concerned with a straight forward story line at all. As we know, Blier does not all together destroy the traditional film narrative, but redefines it, establishes the ensuing mood early on in a film so that the viewer therefore accepts whatever will come later on, no matter how ludicrous and surrealistic. In Merci La Vie he seems to go further than ever in destroying and then playfully reconstructing what a film is. It is both a cinema revolution in one sitting, and a celebration of all that is great and stupid about the movies. Of course, as always with Blier, it is about much more besides.

Charlotte Gainsbourg plays Camille, a teenager living in a quiet seaside town. One day, when at the beach pushing a trolley full of objects and oddly relaxed seagulls, she comes across Joelle (Anouk Grinberg), a young woman in a wedding dress who has just been beaten up and left by her boyfriend. Camille picks her up and puts her in the trolley, taking her home so she can recuperate. Pretty soon Joelle's wild side is revealed, and rather speedily the pair go out into the world to experience what life has to offer... and not all of it is good. Various characters come in and out of the plot, while the two girls find themselves in various eras, all indicated by a change in the colour of the lens. Among the supporting cast is Gerard Depardieu who plays Dr Worms, a medical researcher who has invented a sexually transmitted disease and infected Joelle with it so that he can be credited with finding its cure. And this, believe it or not, is one of the tamest parts of the film.

The whole thing is more of an experience than what we would usually call a film, a series of wonderfully directed vignettes connected by their absurdity. Though featuring its share of disturbing imagery, and scenes modern viewers might find offensive, it's miraculous that Blier's film is as funny as it is and remains a true comedy, albeit a post-modern one. What enriches Blier's parodying though is the fact that it lacks cynicism. Blier may be an intellectual, a critic of society and mankind, but he is not one jaded by humanity, or for that matter what is left of it. He remains curious about people, about human behaviour and failings, and is fearless when approaching isms and conflict. Some may read Merci La Vie as a meditation on feminism, or perhaps more to the point an unflinchingly brutal account of what the female has to put up with in society. It's all here, often in comic but sometimes blunt style; the abusive father, the beating husband, the intimidation of the male gaze. The two girls are at the centre of the film, though Anouk Ginberg's Joelle swings from strong modern woman to submissive old fashioned wife, one minute the manipulator of the male, the next the victim of his chauvinism. By going back and forth loosely and without constraints, Blier's surrealist style

avoids preaching or side taking. It's simply presenting problems, and Merci La Vie has plenty of those to show off.

Indeed, there is much more explored here than male-female problems; let us not forget, that when the film first starts to go back in time at regular intervals, we are faced with the Nazis and their terrible regime. They first appear audibly only, the stomp of their boots through the French streets like a thunder storm about to cause serious bother. "Who are they?" someone asks. "The Germans," comes the reply, followed by an inquisitive, "Are they the ones who killed the Jews?" There are certainly some unsettling scenes involving the Nazis, especially the scene when much of the cast are stripped nude, put in train bunkers and then machine gunned to the ground. But Blier immediately lets his main characters escape this hell. One of them reminds another that it's only a movie, while there is a wish to be in better films, "American films", and the suggestion that they go to Hollywood. They do end up there, but Jean Carmet, after reflecting on his career as a supporting actor, sits catatonic in his wheel chair while America's youth skateboards around him. It's the final shot of a film which brings together AIDS and the SS, causing one character to shout in frustration, "What era are we in now?"

This could be interpreted as cubist filmmaking, life seen from every angle, in every colour, every tinted tone, every viewpoint, every mood, even every time period. It's mind boggling for the first thirty minutes, but one quickly accepts and begins to be perversely addicted to Blier's blending of reality, fantasy, the current and the flashback, all with knowing touches of humour. When the film goes into a blue tinged sequence recalling past events, someone even asks, "Is this a flashback?" It's the ultimate de-construction of cinema. Some may have observed Blier's films becoming more fragmented through the 80s, moving from the anarchic non-logic of Going Places, Get Out Your Handkerchiefs and Buffet Froid, towards the more Godardian likes of Too Beautiful For You. While the latter film was focused on l'amour fou, highlighting Gerard Depardieu's character's predicament at having to choose between a beautiful wife and a dowdy but irresistible secretary, Merci La Vie sets itself much wider. After all, "life" is in the title, and Blier's view of existence is one of madness, chaos and dark beauty.

Merci La Vie was nominated for various Cesars, though was robbed of Best Film in my view. Reviews were good and the film did well across the world, mainly because Depardieu's fame was at its height in the wake of Green Card and Cyrano de Bergerac, two films which brought him a wider audience outside Europe. Time Out wrote "Is it all really happening, or just a movie, or simply Camille's dream? Snazzily shot, wittily performed and structured, Buñuel-fashion, according to the logic of a dream, this bizarre blend of road movie, comedy, psychodrama and various other genres shifts with wayward glee not only between times - the present (?) and WWII - but between colour, black-and-white and monochrome tints. Lending some coherence is a sense that every age has its crises (AIDS, the Holocaust), that life is shit; but Blier's precise intentions are finally unfathomable."

Empire Magazine, failing to see the point in coming up with a synopsis (wisely perhaps), liked the film, but were rather misguided in thinking that Blier's views were possibly the same as those held by his misogynist characters. "Whether the pair ultimately win over the excuses for manhood in this film or are merely rather gutsier victims than most, and whether the misogyny on display is Blier's or that of his characters is not entirely clear. Offensive it may be, but driven at a cracking pace - through image shifts from black-and-white to colour, through period changes from present day to the Occupation, and through cultural references from the war to AIDS - Merci La Vie is still an undeniably exciting, often funny, and thought-provoking ride."

In my opinion, Merci La Vie is one of the finest films ever to have come out of France and I believe it's a shame it isn't more widely appreciated as the game changer it should have been. Comparisons may be made to Bunuel and Godard, but Blier is his own man, a total artist in the truest sense, and totally individual. Merci La Vie, for anyone who has seen it, brings cinema up a level, into a totally different realm that makes one question the importance and value of narrative and clichéd plot developments. Is there a need for formula in art? Is there room for conventions and predictabilities? Not in the world of Bertrand Blier's tremendous Merci La Vie, that's for sure.

1, 2, 3 SUN (1993)

In terms of what we can expect from Bertrand Blier (something of a contradiction in itself, given that Blier's films thrive on the unexpected)

1, 2, 3, Sun is a typically off beat drama not without its (very) black humour.

Among the cast in this wonderful little film is the late and great Marcello Mastroianni as a drunken Italian immigrant, father of numerous children and nuisance in general. All the performances are brilliant, but for his marvellous work on this film (available on DVD across the world) Marcello was awarded the Volpi Cup Award for Best Supporting Actor at the Venice Film Festival.

Rather obscure, often overlooked, this is a film which may at times be a little outrageous and off putting for more easily shocked viewers, but is an essential film for fans of European art cinema. A truly memorable experience.

HOW MUCH DO YOU LOVE ME? (2005)

A relatively recent Blier film is 2005's How Much Do You Love Me?, a typically unpredictable erotic drama about a man (Bernard Campan) who meets a gorgeous prostitute, played by Monica Bellucci. He promises to pay her 100,000 euros a week if she will move in with him. Agreeing to the deal, she moves in. Along the way his doctor dies of a heart attack at the sight of Bellucci's perfect body, and it is revealed that she has a boyfriend, a burly gangster played by Gerard Depardieu.

How Much Do you Love Me? is not quite as sharp as Buffet Froid and Blier's earlier work, but it is still very funny and full of unexpected twists and turns. Campan and Depardieu are both brilliant, but the show is stolen by Bellucci, who is both stunning and hugely charismatic. As the ultimate object of desire, she is empowered in her beauty, a role that could not be further from her iconic turn in the dark Irreversible. She quietly dominates the film with her undeniable beauty, and it's impossible to imagine anyone else in the role.

This is another jagged and biting comic drama from the master Blier which should not be missed.

AN INTERVIEW WITH
BERTRAND BLIER

Here is my Q and A with Bertrand Blier, not only my personal favourite French director, but a man I deem to be one of the world's finest. Here he speaks about working with his father Bernard Blier, Gerard Depardieu and Marcello Mastroianni, as well as some of his most acclaimed films.

The first film I saw of yours, Bertrand, was Buffet Froid. I immediately became comfortable and excited by the style. What kind of experience was Buffet Froid, working with Gerard and your father in one film?

This film was very hard to realise. All of the people I proposed the film to said it was absolutely crazy, nobody would go and see it... so, don't do it. But, I fought very hard and did it. It took a long time but was an easy film to do because of the script and actors.

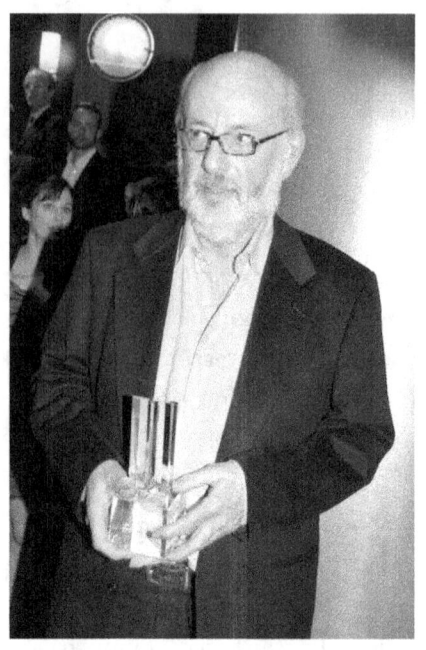

All I had to do was to put the camera in the right place and say "Action". Working with my father was not a problem, more like a reward; and Gerard, with whom I have worked many times, is just like my cousin or uncle

If I can ask about Going Places I would be so pleased. That is still such a wild and exciting film. Was it difficult adapting your own book to the screen and working with the

three lead actors when they were so fresh and inexperienced?

It was a great memory (les Valseuses). When I transposed my book to film I wrote three different scripts which I found interesting, each one written with different coloured ink to use for the film. It's not important whether it's a book or film, it's the same.

We were all young and inexperienced as were the people in the film. It needed young actors who were not 'box-office', so it was perfect to use Depardieu and Deware

Get Out Your Handkerchiefs remains a masterpiece to me. How did the idea of this film originate? Was it a difficult film to make? It is very multi layered and complex.

It was difficult to make, like many other films, and it is always a miracle to end up with a film as good as you imagined it to be. Thank you for the compliments, I see that you have good taste.

I have to say my favourite film of yours is Merci La Vie. I find it so liberating, the way it dispenses with logic and parodies cinema. I imagine this was quite a difficult film to make with the locations, actors, changes in colour and black and white. I have seen a lot of behind the scenes videos and it seems to have been a fun film to make despite the challenges, almost like a party in some ways. Where did the idea for this film come from?

When I was older, about ten or fifteen years later I was in a hotel room in the States. I asked myself if I could re-write a film like 'les Valseurs'. And I came to the conclusion that it would be impossible unless I used two girls instead of boys. Girls who were dangerous and who broke up everything… i.e. their lives and everyone else's. I wrote the script from beginning to end and came back to Paris with the finished script. Everyone said that it would cost a lot of money to realise, and I said "yes, it would be expensive"… But we did it.

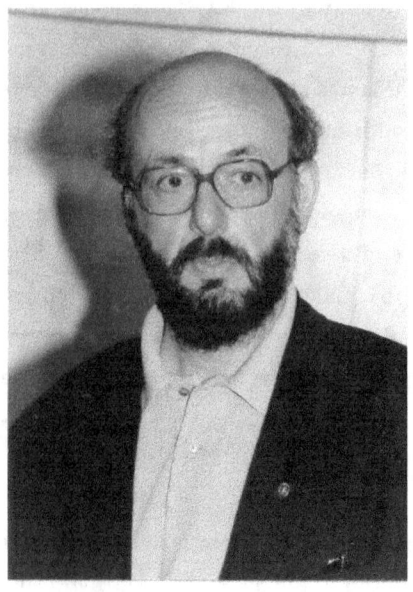

Too Beautiful For You is possibly the ultimate film about the madness of love. I love how Schubert's music invades the soundtrack. Given the character's obsession with Mozart in Get Out Your Handkerchiefs, what is your view on the relationship between music and film, how a soundtrack often manipulates the viewer? Is this something you've been interested in playing around with?

We were very lucky with this film because we had a marvellous composer called Franz Schubert who came (?) to make the music. He was a little bit sad and depressed, but with Depardieu we had a few jokes and drinks with him, and he became more friendly. I also had a good contact with Mozart in a film before. It's important to take good Musicians. It's true that he was sad and getting on our nerves. But, as I say, the Music was just as important as the actors. You have to chose carefully, except the music cannot be done again but the actors can, and the takes can be re-done, but Schubert "non". Just like love, you have to work with it.

Gerard Depardieu is one of my very favourite actors, but Marcello Mastroianni is the one actor whose work affects me the most. What was it like working with him on 1, 2, 3 Sun? I think that is a very overlooked film compared to some of your others.

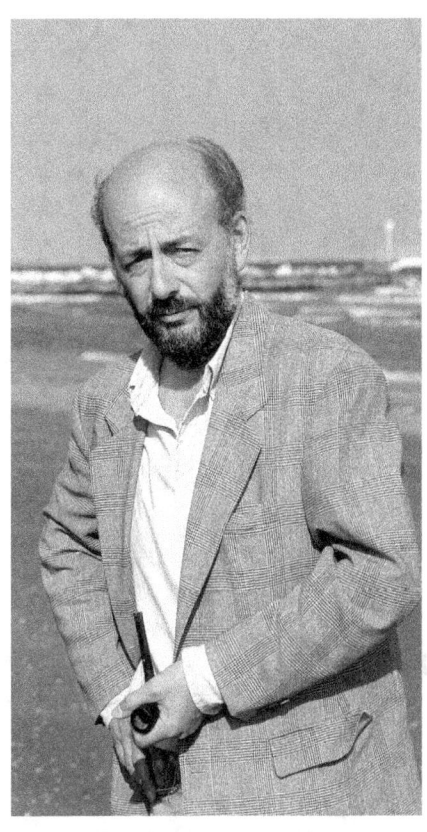

Depardieu is a great actor, but Mastroianni is a great actor and also an exceptional man, which is sometimes not the case with Depardieu. Depardieu is, as I said, a great actor but sometimes difficult... However, he's like a brother or a friend. Mastroianni is always pleasant and charming so my fondest memories are of working with him. It is a shame that we started late, we should have started sooner.

How Much Do You Love Me is another film I really love. How did you come up with this great idea and how was the filming process with Bellucci and Depardieu?

The question is "how did I get the idea?" I was known for working and for being a director for films about "bad boys" etc. So the idea was to steal an actress well known for her beauty and fashion sense and in demand, but someone who was not in my actor's 'Stable'. It's a film about a prostitute used by a stupid imbecile. Belluci and Depardieu working together were very irresistibly funny.

To finish off, can I ask when we might expect to see your next film?

Very soon, I hope. You have to 'organise' a film of course. Maybe 1 ½ to 2 years.
END...

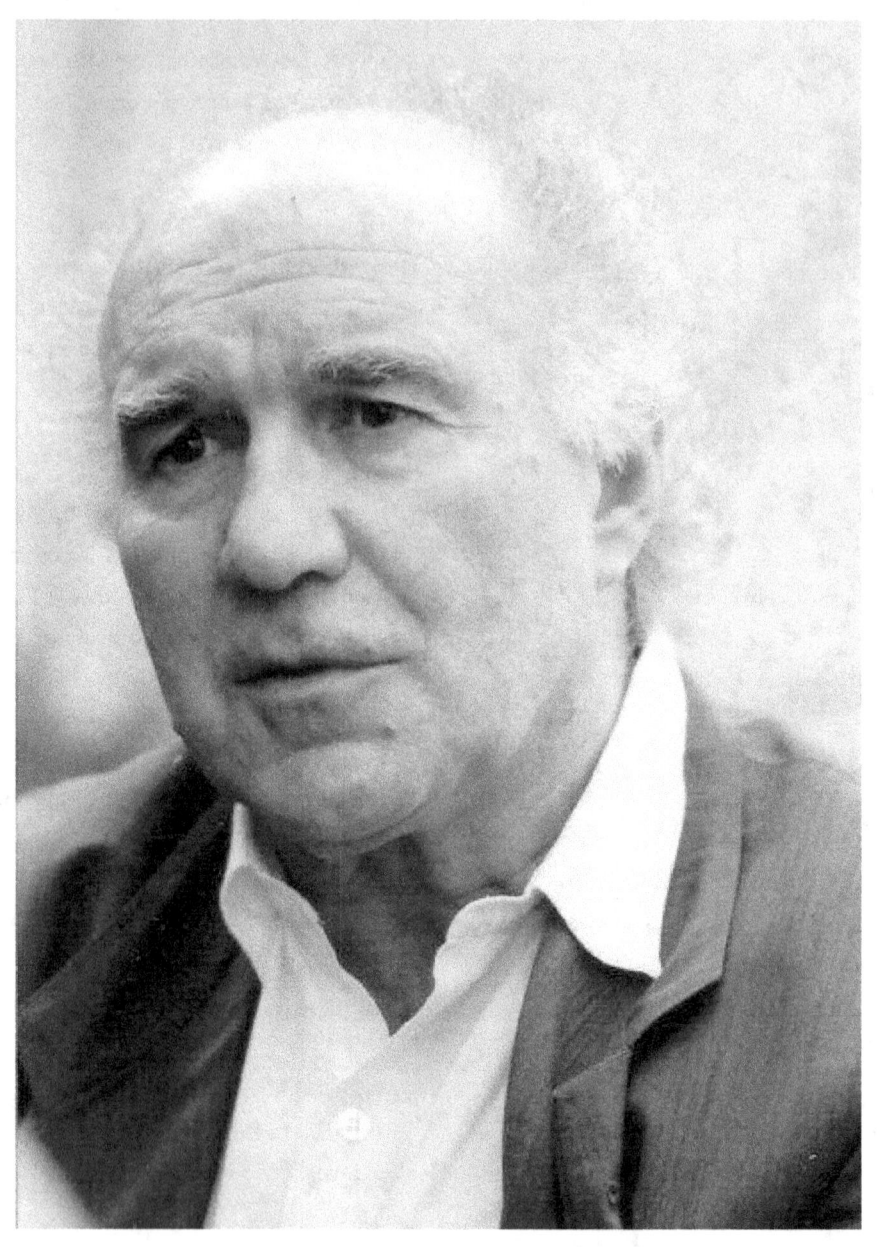

MICHEL PICCOLI

REMEMBERING THE LEGENDARY FRENCH ACTOR

Michel Piccoli, the French actor who sadly passed away in 2020, left behind a sizeable legacy in world cinema. Looking through the vast list of his credits reveals multiple masterpieces, landmark films from each era he acted in, and also the fact he worked with some of the greatest filmmakers in history; from Alfred Hitchcock and Manoel de Oliveira, to Luis Bunuel and Marco Ferreri. He was the most long lasting and reliable staple of French cinema. Piccoli was a man who often propped up a film in a supporting role, making his subtle mark and sometimes stealing the whole thing from everyone else. When he took on a larger lead role, he was equally brilliant. He was a man who admitted he never took a commercial choice in his life, which is not only admirable, but sadly very rare in the film world. "It is for this reason," he says, "that for many years I have worked without an agent."

Here I explore the highlights of his marvellous life on film...

The first time Piccoli worked with Luis Bunuel was on 1956's Death in the Garden. It's one of the oddest Bunuel films, in that it mixes adventure with his usual unique surreal humour, and also the fact it's a transitional film in itself, being released before Bunuel really

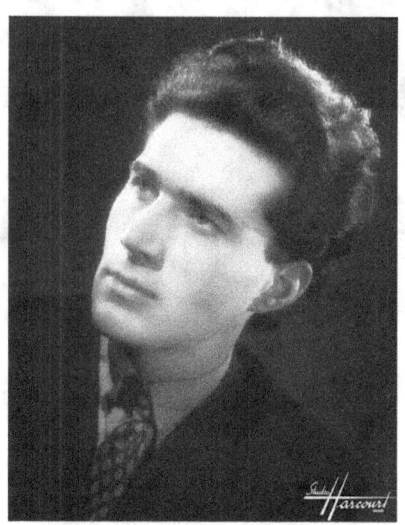

established himself as one of the truly great directors. Piccoli plays a priest in a group of outlaw fugitives who are forced to move into the jungle to survive during a revolution. This is very early Piccoli of course but he is as fascinating to watch as ever. Speaking of Bunuel, who obviously had a fondness for Piccoli given how many times he cast him, Piccoli had only good words about the master: "He taught me to be modest and to have a sense of humour. Generally, he didn't really like actors, but he loved being surrounded by an acting troupe. You were cast based on your personality, not because you were famous."

In 1963 he worked for Jean Luc Godard, alongside Brigitte Bardot, in the seminal French film Contempt, which was without question his breakthrough part. He plays Paul, a playwright who having experienced success in Italy writing for the comedian Toto takes on the task from an American producer (Jack Palance) to rewrite Fritz Lang's version of Odyssey, which he finds pretentious and hard to grasp in his crude manner. Bardot plays Camille, his wife, who comes with him to the famous Cinecitta - a studio once glorious but which has by now seen better days - in Rome to begin rewrites on the film. Unexpectedly, things begin to immediately change between the couple as the project gets underway.

It's difficult perhaps to understand just how radical Godard's films were in the 1960s and just how much of a stir Contempt created. Nearly sixty years on, from its rich visuals and revolutionary direction, to the

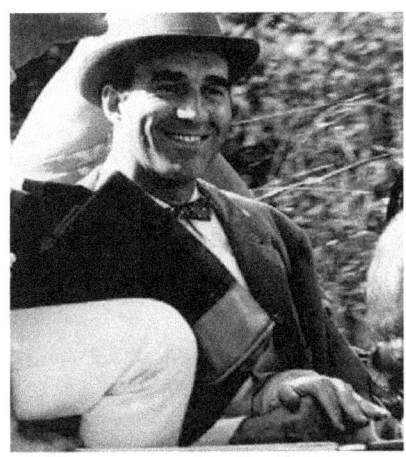

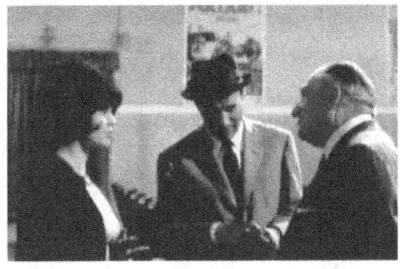

powerful performances and unforgettable soundtrack, it is without doubt a standout film of the decade. Piccoli, it must be said, is marvellous as the writer struggling with the concept that he just might have sold out., while Bardot is beyond iconic, Palance is outrageously obnoxious and Lang quietly impressive. From Piccoli's 250 or so credits, it's among the most vital.

This is a film about compromise, the battle between art and commerciality, the idea of an artist getting lost in the mainstream system which simplifies everything for the masses.

He worked with Bunuel again in Diary of a Chambermaid, released in 1964. Starring Jeanne Moreau as a maid who becomes a sort of obsession of many people around her, her beauty brings about various incidents as she arrives in the country from Paris to work for a well to do family. Piccoli, with slicked back hair and a little moustache, disappears into his role as Monteil, a lecherous chap with a fondness for hunting both game and women.

Of Bunuel he said: "He is a master for many people, a master who I was also lucky enough to have as a friend. He was a man who frightened a lot of people - producers and public - with his way of treating subjects, which was very unorthodox."

Piccoli then had a supporting role in Jacques Demy's The Young Girls of Rochefort (1967). He played a shopkeeper who was also the ex fiancée of the two Rocheford girls, another small part but one which added poignancy to the mix. Even his song and dance number (dubbed as he is) works brilliantly.

Michel worked once again for the great Bunuel in Belle de Jour (1967), alongside Catherine Deneuve as the ice cold woman who, dreaming of erotic fantasies by day, begins to work at a high class whore house at night. Piccoli's role is small, but also vital. He is the man who gives her that look at the ski resort which displeases her, and he is also in the dream sequence where she has shit flung at her. Later in the film, he returns as a client at the whore house. Piccoli represents the "male" as predator, a threatening beast who, not directly of course, is one of the contributing factors to Severine's cold exterior. Bunuel knew he could rely on Piccoli for certain roles, and here he excels in another supporting turn which is deceptively important to the film's development.

Deneuve and Piccoli were back together again for La Chamade (1968), based on the book by Francoise Sagan. She plays Lucile, a seemingly care free young woman who is the mistress of the wealthy businessman Charles, played by Michel Piccoli. Deneuve is irresistible as the woman choosing between a young lover who cannot provide and an older man who offers security. Piccoli is understated and effective as the man who knows he has to be patient for the girl he loves so dearly. The film is often skimmed over in retrospectives of 1960s French cinema, but it remains essential viewing.

In 1969 he took on the lead role in Alfred Hitchcock's Topaz (1969). Hitchcock was famously a huge fan of Bunuel's work and even expressed envy at some of the great man's shots. It seemed natural then that he should cast Bunuel's favourite actor, Piccoli, in a premier part. It may not be one of Hitchcock's finest pictures, and indeed is rather messy in parts, but Michel is boldly brilliant.

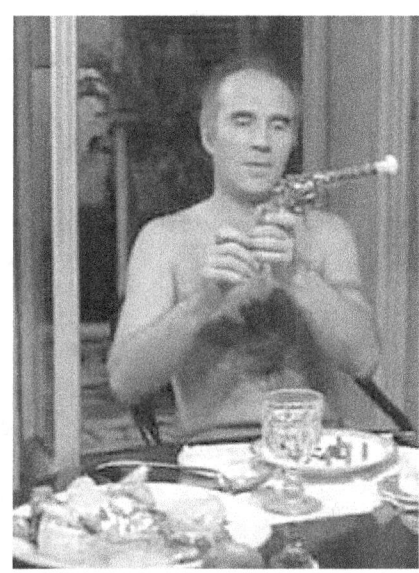

Marco Ferreri made some of the most controversial films of the 1970s, but a year before that decade began he directed the brilliant Dillinger is Dead (1969), one of the edgiest Italian pics of the day.

The film stars Michel Piccoli as Glauco, a designer of gas masks who has become alienated from the world outside and disenfranchised from his profession. While his wife is ill in bed one night, he decides to make himself a more elaborate meal and looks around for ingredients for this grand banquet. He then finds an old gun wrapped up in a newspaper telling of the death of John Dillinger. As the evening goes on, the man becomes increasingly disturbed, painting the gun in a fancy manner and passing the time with music and TV, leading towards a shocking climax that is typical of Ferreri's often outrageous finales.

Though La Grande Bouffe would become Marco Ferreri's great commercial hit, many people insist Dillinger is Dead is his most lasting cinematic statement. And in many ways it is. The tale of a loner, it predates films like Taxi Driver, often seen as the ultimate outsider male misadventure, by a few years. And believe it or not, Dillinger is Dead comes across as more disturbing, more claustrophobic, for the main character doesn't choose to vent his frustration on the scum of the streets, but stays home instead, binging on junk television and rich food before performing his nihilistic release. This is not a satire on society, but a satire on the individual and the nest he makes for himself, cut off from the

107

world outside. It makes for an even more suffocating portrait of loneliness.

According to Piccoli, Ferreri's directorial guidance was loose. As in other movies he made with Ferreri, Piccoli was encouraged to take the part where he wanted. "Ferreri didn't direct me for a second during the shoot; he would simply give spatial indications. It was up to me to play this solitary person, this solitude, this eternal child or this childlike rebirth of mature man, between despair, suicide, simple insomnia, dream."

Dillinger is Dead is a perfect marriage of director and actor, but not as puppet master and puppet. It is, in many ways, a total collaboration. One feels the presence of Ferreri in the mood, but it is up to Piccoli to keep the viewer hooked, and that he achieves with a brilliant performance. Dillinger is Dead is a hugely underrated and very important picture that deserves to be highlighted more often.

Piccoli started the new decade off with The Things of Life (1970), opposite Romy Schneider. Directed by Claude Sautet, it concerns Piccoli as Pierre, an architect who suffers a car crash and then begins to see the life he has lived, and indeed will go on to live, through different eyes. As was often said of Piccoli, he did not think a supporting role or cameo beneath him, but admirers of his work are certainly pleased when he gets to carry a picture as he does here. The New Yorker, who found the film inferior to the likes of Contempt, said of Piccoli "the leading man holds our gaze; confident, and manly, removing his cigarette only to speak his lines." Such a quote only reaches the exterior of what Piccoli does on screen, but it does summarise his simple appeal. Indeed, what is it about Piccoli that makes him so watchable? It is definitely something to do with film magic, though he himself would certainly not have used such a lofty term.

In Bunuel's The Discreet Charm of the Bourgeoise (1972) he had a role which was perhaps his strongest in any Bunuel movie. The picture, which won an Oscar for Best Foreign Film (Bunuel, over seventy by then, famously went to collect his award in a ludicrous wig), concerns a group of pompous upper middle class sorts who, despite their attempts to get together for a dinner party, repeatedly have their plans ruined by some unexpected occurrence. Playful yet also darkly surreal, for some it is the pinnacle of Bunuel's career, where he got it all right and most sharply satirised all the elements of the middle class society he so despised. For me it's a serious contender for ultimate Bunuel, up there with Tristana, un Chein Andalou and L'age Dor, though it has a latter day contender, for me at least, with his final film, That Obscure Object of Desire. Piccoli, once again, is solid, the ultimate Bunuelian man, able to both poke fun at and embody the bourgeois sort he so held in contempt.

He starred once again for Ferreri in La Grande Bouffe (1973). The ultimate tale of indulgence, it featured Piccoli alongside Mastroianni, Ugo Tognazzi and Philippe Noiret, as four over privileged men eating and screwing themselves to death. Piccoli, it must be said, had the most memorable death scene of his career.

Claude Chabrol's Wedding in Blood (1973) remains a vitally important film of 1970s French cinema, and is one of Piccoli's most impressive leading roles of the era. He plays the deputy mayor of a small town who begins an affair with the mayor's wife, played by the sexy Stephane Audran. The affair however gets out of hand and they prove they will do anything to keep their tryst going, even murdering those who get in the way.

Piccoli then had one of the lead roles in Claude Sautet's landmark French film, Vincent, Francois, Paul and the Others (1974). The story follows four friends, and Piccoli's character is a man whose ideals have gone out of the window. Co starring alongside the fresh faced Gerard Depardieu and the veteran legend Yves Montand, it remains a classic of the era but for some reason is not widely available, which seems a crime for such a major picture. It was released the same year as The Phantom of Liberty (1974), his final collaboration with Luis Bunuel, though it was only a brief role. That said, the film itself is vintage Bunuel.

Piccoli then took a role alongside Marcello Mastroianni for the 1976 adaptation of Leonardo Sciascia's novel Todo Modo by Elio Petri. A key Italian film of the seventies, it was recently restored in all its glory, though a vintage print is what I viewed. The film, a typically socio-political and theological drama from Petri, concerns Marcello Mastroianni as Don Gaetano, a priest overseeing the gathering of Christian Democrats who are on a religious retreat during an epidemic, one of whom is Piccoli. (The opening shot of one of the main characters being driven through an Italy in lock down proves eerily prophetic - as I write this during the coronavirus nightmare.) While there, holed up in various sealed rooms decorated with heavy religious iconography and paintings, the politicians attempt to cleanse themselves of past sins. But things start to turn towards the unexpected when each man begins to die one after the other.

Piccoli had an uncredited cameo in Ettore Scola's That Night in Varennes (1982), playing the role of King Louis XVI. The film is about a group of well-to-do rich folk who get caught up in the French revolution while all travelling cross country in a stagecoach together. At nearly three hours, Scola manages to keep the film interesting with imaginative direction and camera shots which bring us intimately among the bright and vibrant, though often painfully flawed, characters. He is aided of course by an ensemble of fine actors.

Two landmark performances came in the early 1980s; firstly in Marco Bellochio's A Leap in the Dark, a role which won him the Best Actor gong at Cannes; secondly in Strange Affair, which earned him the Silver Bear for Best Actor. The eighties as it happens were a kind of later golden period for Piccoli. He was back, after twenty years, with Jean Luc Godard once again for his landmark Passion (1982). It received a lot of acclaim, and Piccoli's work was much celebrated. This time he wasn't playing the writer, but the producer, one sporting a chronic cough. Very much a follow up to Contempt, it explored once again the constraints and pressures of art and the creative act.

I feel the need however, to highlight lesser known films which deserve just as much acclaim. One of Piccoli's personal favourites, and one he produced, was Luciano Tovoli's directorial curiosity, The General of the Dead Army. One of the most interesting and unexpectedly enjoyable films from Italian cinema in the 80s, Marcello Mastroianni stars as a general, believed at first to be an honourable professional, who is sent by the widow of a colonel (played by Anouk Aimee) to retrieve her husband and his troops' remains from Albania, all of whom died in World War 2. Accompanied by a Chaplain played by Michel Piccoli,

the general heads out with his crew to unearth the bones. However, as the Chaplain learns, Mastroianni likes the booze a little too much and as the film goes on, he gets drunker and drunker, while also becoming infatuated with the widow of the colonel. Worse still, he becomes jealous of the deceased colonel, dreams of Anouk in the night, and in the end resorts to an act so desperate, and also so genuinely funny in how Mastroianni acts it out, that one can only laugh.

The odd thing about The General of the Dead Army is that it begins, and seems for the early part, to be a serious examination of loss and war, with the aftermath of combat being just as tragic as the losses made on the battlefield. However, quite early on it develops a comedic edge that makes it a refreshing film. Piccolo and Mastroianni work off each other wonderfully, while Marcello is genuinely brilliant as the unhinged general, who may just have a bit too much power for his own good - and of course for the good of everyone around him. Piccolo has a quiet dignity about him, especially in the face of Marcello's burping drunken general.

Unsurprisingly, given the way the Italian army is presented here, the film received little fan fare upon release and only appeared in a limited amount of theatres. Tovoli co wrote the film with Piccoli, which suggests it was a real labour of love for them and not something they went into with commercial expectations any way; still, it's a shame it isn't better known. Extremely obscure and overlooked, though available on DVD in what is a nice release with English subtitles, it may be a bit uneven but it certainly is entertaining, well acted and wonderfully directed despite its niggling flaws.

Michel Deville's Death in a French Garden (1985) is a definite stand out in a heavily prolific decade. It follows Christopher Malavoy as a guitar teacher who starts having an affair with the mother of his latest student. Nicole Garcia plays Julia, the mother

with whom David becomes involved. Michel Piccoli is her husband, Graham, someone we distrust from the start and understand may know more about their little affair than he lets on. Richard Bohringer also has a notable role as a hitman who befriends David, and has his eye on an artefact in Graham's possession.

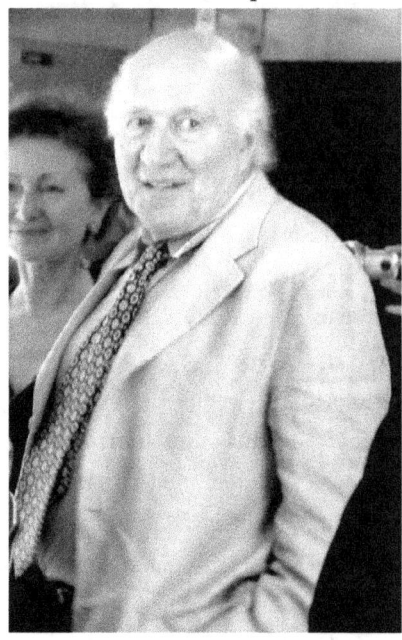

Death in a French Garden is a wonderfully subtle thriller, full of murky imagery, sharply defined characters and twists which are more believable and organic than over the top. The acting is superb, from Anemone as the camera friendly neighbour with a walking stick, to Piccoli's all-smiles husband who reveals hidden layers towards the film's end. Excellently guided by Deville (who co wrote the script), this is one of the films in Piccoli's massive filmography which deserves a rediscovery.

One of my very favourite Piccoli films is Le Paltroquet (1986), scripted and directed by Michel Deville. A surreal and anarchic film reminiscent of Bertrand Blier, it features Piccoli as a barman named the Nonentity, who resides over the shoddy establishment, run by Jeanne Moreau, who never comes out from behind the bar and constantly sees to her make up, while putting Piccoli down in the process. The bar (if you can call it that) is frequented by four men; a doctor, a tradesman, a journalist and a professor. One night as they play cards a police inspector arrives to say there has been a murder, and he is pointing the finger at not just the four men, but the lady of the night, played by Fanny Ardent, who also frequents the run down watering hole.

Le Paltroquet is one of those satisfyingly strange films, crammed full of surreal imagery and wonderful twists and turns. Indeed, it puts conventional films to shame. The performances too are splendid; Moreau is marvellous as the ageing owner, but Piccoli impresses the most as the almost animal like nonentity, making bizarre sounds and scurrying round after the drinkers in a lowly, often pathetic manner. The final twist however, as unexpected as it is, has him in a more dignified manner.

Piccoli received more praise and a Cesar nomination for his role as Milou in Louis Malle's May Fools (1990). A deceptively light farce concerning a family rowing over a will in a country estate, set against the Paris riots, it was one of Malle's final pictures, as well as one of his finest. Piccoli is genial and charming as the son who desperately wants to hang on to the family home, despite it being a profitless husk. "Please don't take my childhood away!" he says at one point. In the end we are aware, when the family leave after the funeral, that Milou is the only one who hasn't moved on and started his own life outside the estate. The surreal final scene, a dreamy dance with his deceased mother, sadly proves this. It's a very touching performance.

In Jiri Weiss' Martha and I (1991) he put in a splendid effort as Ernst, a Jew who fled the Nazis before the outbreak of World War 2. The story is seen through the eyes of a boy, who observes Ernst marrying his aunt Martha. It's a subtle take on a story that, if made in America, would have been hopelessly melodramatic and schmaltzy. Weiss however keeps things understated, aided as he is by a superb Piccoli in an underrated effort.

The same year's The Children Thief (1991) is an overlooked gem from the early 90s. Based on the book by Jules Supervielle, The Children Thief casts Marcello Mastroianni as Bigua, a rich Argentinean living in France who begins stealing children to put in he

and his wife's expansive home. The film features another charming but paradoxically troubling performance from Marcello, and also has a memorable appearance from Piccoli, who plays Armand, a bushy eye-browed magician type.

One of Piccoli's most gripping performances came in The Beautiful Troublemaker (1991), where he played an artist coming out of retirement. Though the initial released version ran at almost four hours, there was a more commercial version which ran at under two. However, for a truer idea of director Jacques Rivette's vision, the original which aired at Canes is the superior film.

Piccoli plays Frenhofer, a legend in the art world who is forced to do one last painting - by a mysterious yearning within - when he meets a beautiful young woman (played by Emmanuelle Beart) with an exquisite body. Unsurprisingly, the film won the Grand Prix at Cannes and has received a lot of acclaim down the years. Roger Ebert was a huge fan,

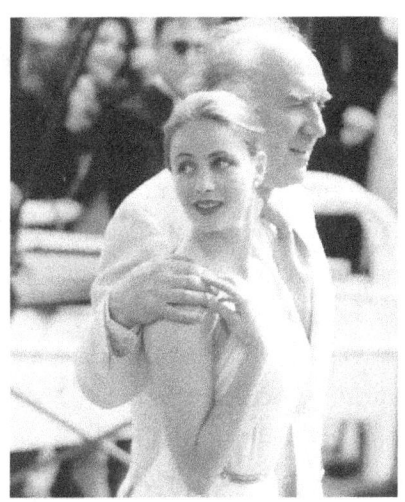

putting it in his Great Movies List back in 2009. As magnetic as Beart is in her role, Piccoli is also compulsively watchable as the ageing painter, stirred by the beauty of the youth before his eyes.

A totally sidelined gem of a film, and one featuring a solid effort from Michel, is Walking a Tight Rope, the 1992 drama about a gay ageing writer who gets fixated on a half Arabic tightrope walker, and uses his influence to further the young man's career. But Piccoli's Maurice is not who he seems and leaves behind him a trail of destruction and a chain of people who are not only obsessed with him but often remain committed to the point that they will sacrifice their lives. A compulsively watchable film, Piccoli is at his best.

Les cent et une nuits de Simon Cinema is in my view one of the best films of the 1990s, directed by the great Agnes Varda from a script of her own. It stars Michel Piccoli in one of his best efforts of the 80s as an eccentric castle dwelling cinema fan who enlists the help of a film student to reclaim the memory he is losing. Rather than looking through old photos however, Simon Cinema insists the student tells him stories from cinema's rich and illustrious past.

A truly joyous film, Varda's homage to the world of movies is a pleasure from start to finish. Marcello Mastroianni plays The Italian Friend, one of the best efforts from his final two years on earth and among his most touching parts. He is not, however, the only film legend that the brilliant Varda managed to get on board this dream project, which exists as a kind of fantasy for cinephiles; the cast also features Robert De Niro, Catherine Deneuve, Gerard Depardieu, Jane Birkin, Jeanne Moreau and Anouk Aimee, among many others.

These days, One Hundred and One Nights is hard to get a hold of, and if one does manage to get it on DVD it will either be expensive or not subtitled into English. However, old copies of the film now out of print are out there in film land and if one can get a hold of it it's well worth the hunt. Now let's lobby for a proper re-release worldwide!

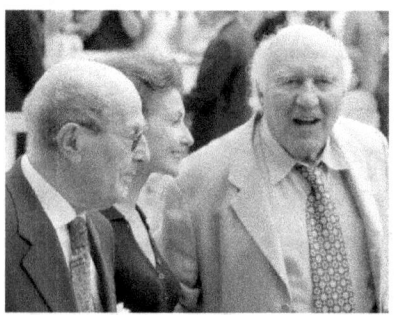

Piccoli worked with the famous Manoel De Oliveira on his 1996 film Party. Though not quite up there with Piccoli's future collaborations with the veteran filmmaker, this engaging film depicting a dinner party is typically well observed, over seen as it is by the keen eye of Manoel.

Travelling Companion (1996), a sadly overlooked gem in Piccoli's career, had him cast opposite Asia Argento. Argento won much acclaim for her role as Cora, a waitress who walks dogs for extra money, and starts a friendship with a client's ageing father suffering from dementia, played by Piccoli, who she is paid to keep tabs on. Piccoli *becomes* the character in a way that is eerily haunting. This does not come across as a piece of work at all, but as Piccoli embodying the ailing gentleman who unexpectedly becomes an important factor in the young girl's life.

Manoel de Oliveira's I'm Going Home (2001) is an understated gem, as appealing and engaging as any of the great man's work, and featuring a seminal performance from a Piccoli at his late peak. He stars as Gilbert Valance, an ageing actor, much respected in his field, who after a triumphant stage performance one night, learns that his wife, daughter and son in law have all died in a car crash, leaving him the sole carer of his 9 year old grandson. We observe Gilbert's life, continuing his stage career and turning down TV roles which he believes, rightly so, are beneath him, but angering his long suffering agent nonetheless. Eventually he accepts a small part in an American film for the director John Crawford (played by John Malkovich). Once on set however, he sees the ludicrous nature of his work (he is wearing a wig, stumbling through English dialogue) and comes to a conclusion about where he is in his life and where he perhaps should be.

Manoel came up with the idea for the film originally when an actor he had been working with left the film set midway through a take to say he was going home for a rest. This got de Oliveira thinking about home as a concept, what it represents and its womb like sense of safety and protection, it being the one place where we can cut off the outside world. Casting Piccoli, one of the world's most respected and longest serving screen actors was an inspired choice. Manoel had directed Marcello Mastroianni in his final film role, in Voyage to the Beginning of the World, shortly before his death, so he had experience in stories about endings, about a life coming to a crossroads. Given the fact that Manoel was 98 when he directed this film makes it even more poignant and quietly moving.

The script is graceful and realistic, while Manoel makes directorial choices few others would. Like Theo Angelopoulos, he is patient with his camera, lingering on shots for longer than you might think possible to reveal truths and hidden depths in the most everyday of situations. Piccoli is simply wonderful in the lead, carrying the film as a man who is alive and electrifying when on stage, but a little off centre, if not unresponsive in the real world. Catherine Deneuve has a brief role in

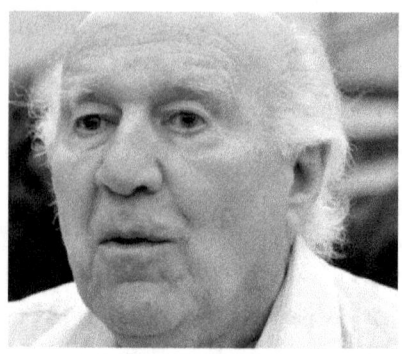

the opening ten minutes as a fellow performer, and she is brilliant in this scene; it's just a shame that her part doesn't expand itself into the main narrative of the film.

I'm Going Home received a lot of acclaim upon release, winning Best Film at Sao Paulo Film Festival and Haifa Film Festival. Admirers of de Oliveira's unique cinema, and the wonderful Piccoli, should definitely seek out this hidden gem.

Piccoli worked with the brilliant de Oliveira again on Belle Toujours (2006), Manoel's sequel to Luis Bunuel's Belle De Jour. An open homage to both the film and Bunuel himself, Manoel's follow up is a typically slow, measured and carefully played story, light on drama but high on poetic poignancy and with a strange, quiet atmosphere of its own.

Piccoli reprises his role of Henri from Belle De Jour. We first see him at a classical music concert. We assume he is with the two women at either side of him, but later learn he is alone. While sent by the beautiful music, he spots a familiar face in the crowd. Seated amongst the other people is Severine herself, here played by Bulle Oglier, a perfectly believable aged version of Severine if not the beautiful Deneuve herself.

Overtaken by the need to get in contact with his old "friend", he follows her round the city, frequenting the bar she goes in and then finding out where she lives. Eventually she agrees to meet up with him for dinner, but what will unfold, and just what is the old man wishing to express?

Piccoli is tremendous in this film, a man constantly expressing quiet amusement with everything around him, an ageing alcoholic haunted by a strange past and spooked further by a short future which awaits him. The film is full of wonderful, simple imagery, with Manoel's camera lingering for long periods to reveal elements of odd beauty. The dinner sequence is one of the most intriguing in Piccoli's rich filmography, lit by candles with a view of a quiet if not dead city outside through the huge window. There is much to be enjoyed here, even in the weird silences. This is a film about age, and the candles act as metaphors for the years the pair have lived, the melting wax a reminder of the little time they have left.

Belle Toujours was deservedly acclaimed upon release. As usual de Oliveira had created a unique experience, somewhere between film and poem, paradoxically unsettling and soothing from start to finish. Anyone looking for a stand out Piccoli effort should head straight to this odd little gem.

Another latter period highlight for Piccoli came in Theo Angelpoulos' startling masterpiece, The Dust of Time (2008). The master's final film, it stars Willem Defoe as a film director of Greek descent who finds a letter his mum wrote to his dad in the fifties, just as his teenaged daughter begins to rebel and go wayward. Piccoli plays his father Spyros, in a film which goes from present day to the 1950s and everywhere in between, charting the way Spyros and his true love Eleni (played by Irene Jacob in all eras) drift in and out of each other's lives before coming together in the 1970s.

Another odyssey, as many of Angelopoulos' films are, it was the second part in an uncompleted trilogy and boasted fine, haunting work from Defoe, Piccoli and another Angelopoulos favourite, Bruno Ganz. It is perhaps Theo's most striking picture, crammed full of unforgettable imagery, moments of poignancy and scenes of haunting beauty. It also features one of his most moving finales, a resurrection of sorts., with Piccoli and his granddaughter running in the snow towards a brighter future.

We Have a Pope (2011) gave Piccoli the ultimate role for a grand old man of cinema, the Pope himself. In Nanni Moretti's gripping drama, he is Cardinal Melville, suddenly and against his wishes appointed the biggest role there is, the pope. As good as the film is, it's impossible to imagine anyone but Piccoli, especially at this stage of his career, playing the role of this reluctant pope. A Multi layered and expertly played effort, it's Piccoli's grand final statement as leading actor in a film which seems to have been made solely for the purpose to give us one last look at what made Michel so special. Acclaimed by critics, the Vatican urged the film to be boycotted. Controversies aside, We Have a Pope deserves to be seen, and is one of the finest films of 21st century Italian cinema.

There were other highlights in the latter period, such as the splendid Boxes, directed by and also starring Jane Birkin, and You Ain't Seen Nothin' Yet, a challenging but ultimately rewarding cinematic experience with an all star cast playing themselves.

I cannot claim to have seen every film featuring Michel Piccoli (after all, he appeared in over 200 if you add up TV movies and regular films) but his is the kind of career that, lo and behold, if he is in the cast then it's more than likely going to be worth your time. He was an ever present face in world cinema, rather like his contemporary Mastroianni, only he lasted another twenty odd years longer than his fallen friend. He worked almost to the very end, giving his all, providing his formidable but comforting presence to any film he found interesting, any director who piqued his interest. It was, he said, more about having passion than talent.

Piccoli died in May 2020, "in the arms of his wife Ludivine and his children Inord and Missia after a stroke." Piccoli leaves behind a void which, it must be said, can never be filled. "I do not put on an act," he once said. "I slip away behind my characters. To be an actor, you have to be flexible,"

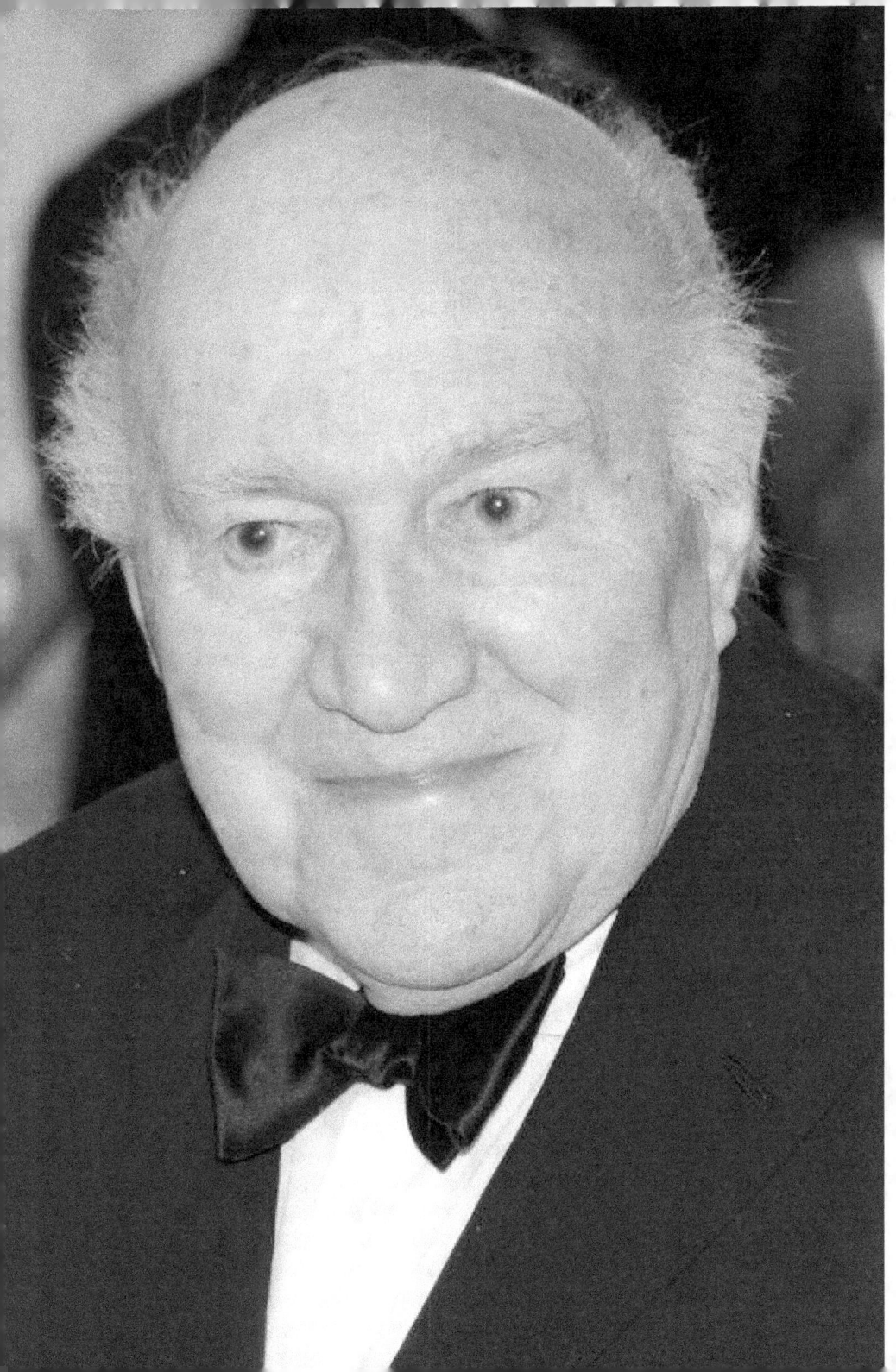

MICHELANGELO ANTONIONI AND THE TRILOGY OF DISCONTENT

CHRIS WADE EXPLORES
ANTONIONI'S SEMINAL
EARLY SIXTIES TRIPTYCH ON
ALIENATION IN THE MODERN
WORLD...

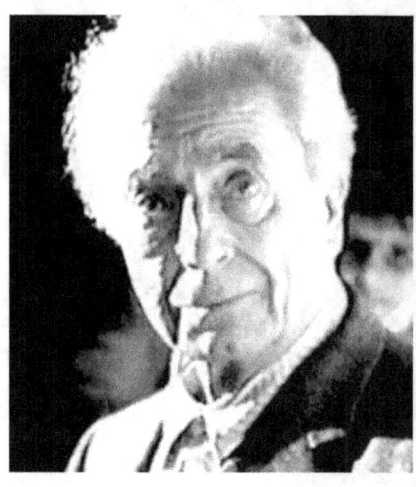

The cinema of Italian director Michelangelo Antonioni is a world of enigma, as mysterious as the paintings of Giorgio De Chirico, but so incomparably unique that Antonioni's moody studies of alienation and misplacement exist in a category of their own. In his final feature film, 1995's Beyond the Clouds, completed with the help of German filmmaker Wim Wenders (Antonioni was unable to communicate due to the after effects of a stroke), John Malkovich plays a film director travelling Europe for inspiration for his next film. This calm, studious man, clearly an alter ego in the truest sense for the reflective Antonioni, utters the immortal words "I didn't discover reality until I started photographing it." He also states that through his whole "career" (for want of a better word, though it does indicate that the filmmaker is both a professional and an artist) all he has really done is capture and enlarge the surfaces of the things around him, as if to try and penetrate them to get to what is underneath. What does it all mean? What is the real meaning? These questions are clichéd, but they run through Antonioni's films repeatedly. He does not come out and ask such questions of course, at least not literally through dialogue, but it is in the way his people are placed, misplaced and displaced, that our own thoughts and confusions about life are reflected.

For some time, especially during the 1960s, Antonioni was one of the most acclaimed directors in the world. He won the Palme d'Or, the Golden Lion, the Golden Leopard and the Golden Bear awards, the only filmmaker to do so in history. An art director in the truest sense, he openly acknowledged the fact that cinema did not always have to be entertainment, that it could mirror literature and even walk hand in hand with it, that shots could and indeed often should linger as long as a writer might pore over a description of a person, a face or a place. His films, reflective and introverted, reflected the angst and frustrations of a generation, in particular his haunting trilogy of what some call discontentment; beginning with L'Avventura (1960), La Notte (1961) and L'Eclisse (1962), three of the most important Italian films of the decade and ones which not only changed the rulebook of art cinema, but also influenced generations of filmmakers to follow. These existential, thought provoking films, a master class in self control and subtlety, cemented Antonioni as a vital force in cinema and introduced a new language into film.

He was born in Ferrara, Italy, in 1912, raised by a well off family who owned land in the region. Michelangelo described his childhood as happy, a warm and intelligent mother and a father who was good and pure, a man born into working class origins who worked hard to make a better life for his young family. Antonioni recalled the freedom of his childhood, playing out with friends, most of whom, he later pointed out, were poor, and he was drawn to them for their purity.

Explaining this to Aldo Tassone, Michelangelo stated, "The poor still existed at that time, you recognized them by their clothes. But even in the way they wore their clothes, there was a fantasy, a frankness that made me prefer them to boys of bourgeois families. I always had sympathy for young women of working-class families, even later when I attended university: they were more authentic and spontaneous."

He was a creative and artistic child, drawn to music and drawing. A young violinist, Antonioni gave it up when he discovered film as a teenager. When it came to art it seems vital that even at such a primitive point he did not like to draw people or figures, but buildings, streets, organising them into imaginary towns. As he noted, these sketches "were like little films", though they were not occupied by human beings. This is of course fitting. Antonioni always had a fascination with architecture, structure and the solid nature of a person's surroundings, and the fact people came secondary in these early drawings suggests he always had chosen the certainty of buildings and streets, in all their shapes, to the uncertainty of the individual who roamed them.

He graduated from Bologna's university with qualifications in economics but began writing for a newspaper, Il Corriere Padano, in 1935, then moving on to Rome where he wrote for the Fascist film magazine, Cinema, which had been formed and edited by Mussolini's son Vittorio. He didn't last long there however and after being let go, so to speak, he began to study film, not with a view of commentating on the medium but becoming an active practiser of it. His first step into cinema came during the war years when he co-wrote A Pilot Returns with Roberto Rossellini. He also worked as assistant to Enrico Fulchignoni on his film I due Foscari, and in 1943 as assistant to Marcel Carne on Les visiteurs du soir. His first steps as a filmmaker in his own right were in part-documentary,

124

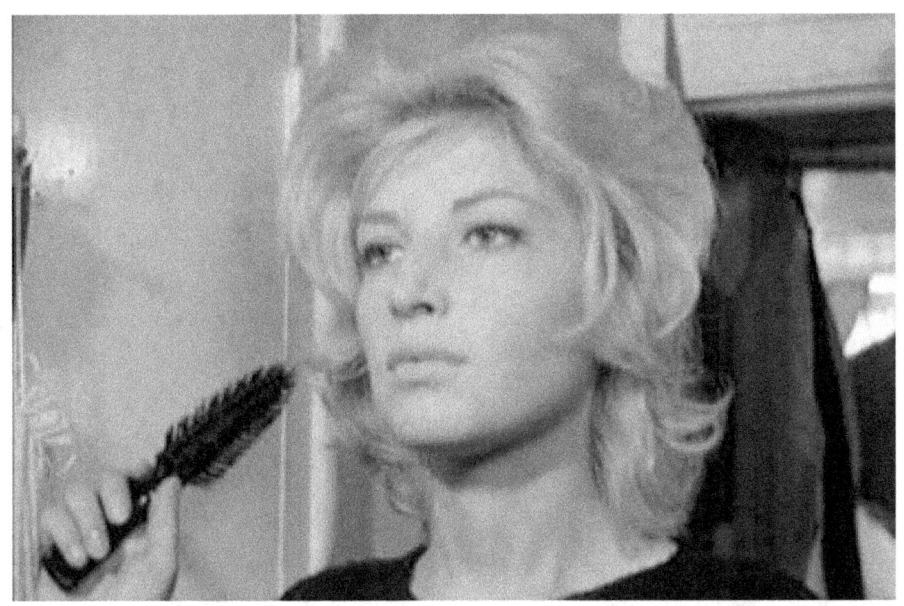

when he filmed some neorealist short portraits of working families. His career was stalled however when he acted as part of the Italian resistance during World War 2, narrowly avoiding being put to death during the conflict.

His film debut saw him move away from the kind of neorealism perfected by the likes of Vittorio De Sica and into exploring the dichotomies of the middle classes, Cronaca di un amore (1950) being a stand out in this era of Italian cinema.

Through the fifties he continued to make films, establishing his style and sharpening his approach. What they all had in common was a concern for the middle classes, a world he knew much better and could see from within, rather than having to look at the poor and working classes through the scrutinizing lens of an outsider. His movies became intellectual studies of alienation, like The Vanquished (1952) and The Girlfriends (1955). Only The Outcry, made in 1957, went back to the earthier concerns of neorealism, focusing on a factory worker. Still, despite its focus being elsewhere on a class level, it was still a meditation on displacement.

It wasn't until 1960 though that Antonioni's individual style became world renowned, with the release of the masterpiece, L'avventura.

L'AVVENTURA (1960)

L'Avventura, like Fellini's La Dolce Vita of the same year, was one of the truly heroic, iconic master works of Italian cinema in the sixties. Michelangelo Antonioni had already made a name for himself to a certain degree in the 1950s, but it wasn't until the 1960s, with minds broadening thanks to the advances of Italian cinematic boundaries, and of course the alternative French New Wave led by Truffaut and Godard, that Antonioni's reflective, inward brand of philosophical cinema could enter the mainstream radar. As much as Italian cinema in the sixties was dominated by Fellini, Antonioni also made some vital movies which act as direct parallels to Federico's lavish pictures. Whereas Fellini's work was psychological in a different manner, in that we were shown the dreams and fantasies of the mind which were projected without question on to the screen, Antonioni rarely let us have a glimpse into what was going on in the heads of his characters. It was up to us to guess, judging by expressions, body language and movement.

L'Avventura is possibly Antonioni's most important work. It is the first part of his tetralogy of alienation, which also included the following year's La Notte (an equally important picture) and L'eclisse Written by Antonioni with Elio Bartolini and Tonio Guerra, the film is another tale of alienation, telling the story of a young woman named Anna, played by Lea Massari who goes missing during a boat ride. Gabriele Ferzetti is Sandro, her lover, who with the girl's friend Claudia, played by the iconic Monica Vitti, go on a quest to search for her. Sandro is a typical Antonioni character, a middle class intellectual not attuned to his inner emotions, in this case an architect, a man concerned with aesthetics and outside appearances, a perfect character-metaphor for Antonioni's disjointed, alienated universe. As one

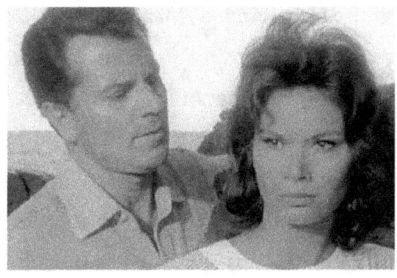

might expect, it is during the search that Sandro starts an affair with the picturesque Claudia, though one can guess from the start that their affair is misguided and ill advised.

Antonioni began shooting the film in August of 1959, wrapping it up in January of 1960. Michelangelo and his crew encountered many problems during filming, and the island sequences shot on Lisca Bianca, which were set to be completed in under three weeks, took a whole four months due to plagues of rats and reptiles, not to mention the unnaturally cold weather. Antonioni must have felt his project was doomed, especially when the naval boat intended to take them back and forth from the island failed to turn up, and the crew had to construct their own rafts to transport filming equipment to and from the so called set.

L'Avventura was also very nearly not completed, when the production company in charge of the film went bankrupt. Antonioni, thankfully hanging on to some film stock of his own, convinced the cast and crew to finish the film without pay. When food dried up for three whole days, the whole crew went on strike, forcing Antonioni and his assistant director to take on all tasks themselves and get to work alone. Thankfully, funding did come back in from another source and, despite the serious hiccups, filming picked back up again.

The film was met with mixed reviews upon release, but soon gathered steam when various fellow filmmakers insisted it was the best picture that had been screened at

Cannes, even though it was met with hostility by the press upon its premiere there. Against all odds, it bagged the Jury Prize at Cannes, not to mention gongs from the BAFTAs, the Golden Globes and various other organisations. Not only did it set the tone of the rest of Antonioni's oeuvre, and his outlook as a filmmaker, but it also raised the bar for European directors and the film industry in itself. While Hollywood was struggling to keep its youth audience with out of touch, socially irrelevant blockbusters and comedies, the Italians and the French were pushing the boundaries and reaching out. Antonioni in particular spoke to the isolated soul, anyone who has been made to feel alienated by society and its expectations of the individual.

La Dolce Vita had reflected empty lives in a so called high society with exuberance and vitality, all of it hiding a void beneath the pretty surface. In L'Avventura, Antonioni didn't bother with the gayety and liveliness of Fellini's world at all, and reflected the barren meaninglessness with gestures and actions. These spoilt people have nothing left inside, no passion, no joy, bored as they are with all they have got and what they more importantly lack. When they fail to find Anna, they also fail to find themselves and a meaning to their bourgeois, empty existence. She becomes a metaphor for their quest for self fulfilment. Antonioni said his film was "expressed through images in which I hope to show not the birth of an erroneous sentiment, but rather the way in which we go astray in our sentiments. Because as I have said, our moral values are old. Our myths and conventions are old. And everyone knows that they are indeed old and outmoded."

L'Avventura is one of the key films of the era, not just in Italian film but cinema as a whole. It is the start of the cinema of alienation, miscommunication, the cinema of looking inward while deluding oneself about the physical reality around us. It is also one of Antonioni's true visual and intellectual masterpieces.

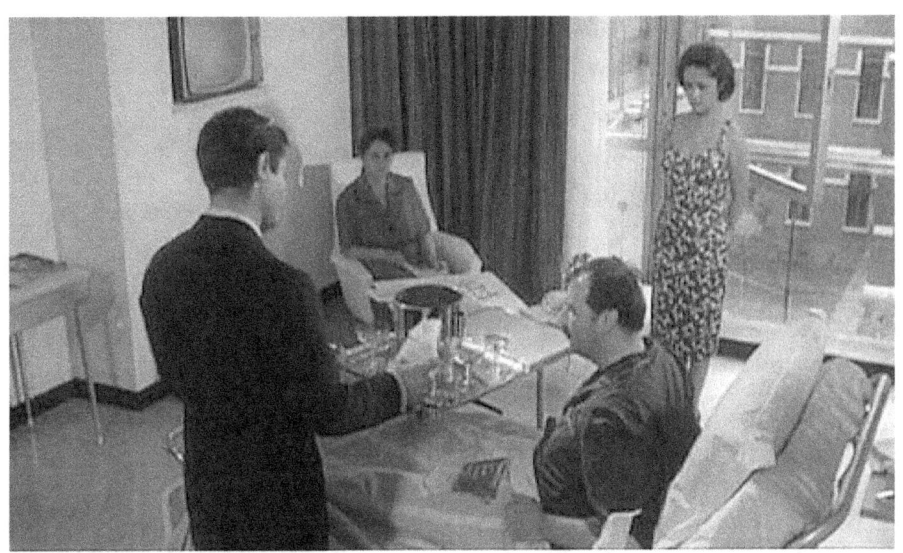

LA NOTTE (1961)

As the fifties turned into the sixties, Antonioni had established himself as the master of existentialism with L'Avventura. When he and Marcello Mastroianni met they were both at the height of their early peaks. La Notte, released in 1961, remains one of the director's seminal films, and indeed, one of the strongest efforts from Marcello from his immediate post-La Dolce Vita success. On a basic level, La Notte is one day in the life of a couple whose relationship is crumbling. Marcello is Giovanni, a writer and intellectual, married to Lidia (Jeanne Moreau). His recent work, a book called The Season, is doing well. When the couple visit their dying friend, who later turns out to have been a more important figure to Lidia than Giovanni, they drink champagne together, though Lidia is too unsettled by his frailty, so near to death, and has to leave. Giovanni is too self-centred to comfort his upset wife, instead staying with the dying friend longer and then having a brief dalliance with a mentally disturbed patient in the next room; worse still, he then tells Lidia all about it, though seems morbidly disappointed that she displays no jealousy.

Upon leaving the hospital they head for a party in his honour. Lidia doesn't stick around for long though, leaving slyly and roaming the more run down streets of Milan where the couple had enjoyed their early years together. As the day goes on the frustrated wife and quietly egotistical intellectual appear to drift apart more and more, heading to a millionaire's party which is lavish but as emotionally empty as the various shindigs in Fellini's La Dolce Vita. Lidia goes off for a while with a man, as the rain pours down, but declines to go a step further, while Giovanni flirts with an infidelity with the millionaire's daughter. They meet up at the end, both realising their love for one another has died. But what will the future hold for them? The final image, of a desperate, clinging Mastroianni kissing Moreau, disinterested and lamenting her dead love for him, remains one of the most haunting and striking shots of cinema.

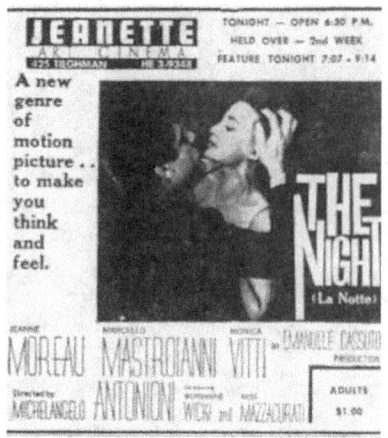

La Notte may be documenting a crumbling relationship, but visually it's one of the most beautiful, full and stylish European films of that or any other era. Though the film is set in 24 hours, it harbours years within its framework, the months that have passed by and seen the couple drifting apart. Giovanni is trying to exist in the moment and enjoy his success, but Lidia is the one carrying the burden. All this is reflected in the careful camera movements and Antonioni's expert eye at portraying quiet disillusionment and alienation.

Though most people look back upon the film as a prime example of Antonioni at his best, and indeed as a showcase for a Mastroianni still glowing from his La Dolce Vita glories, the film in many ways belongs to the sombre Moreau, who is absolutely brilliant in her part. Marcello is excellent too, but the weight of the film - almost by default in the way it's structured - rests on her back, and she carries it firmly and without fault. The subtlety is in Antonioni's hands however, who ensures we never see phony emotional theatrics or tepid sentimentality. These people are unattached to their emotions towards each other (though Mastroianni more so), unable to express themselves in this dire situation, though Moreau finds it easier as her night-long odyssey, her inner journey, gets to its end. Though Moreau gets there in the end, Antonioni proves his point that the lack of open communication can destroy human relationships. This message remains vitally relevant to this day, despite us being in a so called age of communication and openness.

Marcello's vagueness opens the film for Moreau's tortured wife. Quite often in Antonioni's films, the men were closed books while the women were open, the ones we relate to throughout. Addressing this issue, Antonioni said, "One question I am often asked is why the women in my films are more lucid than the men. I was raised among women: my mother, my aunt, and lots of cousins. Then I got married, and my wife had five sisters. I have always lived among women; I know them very well. Speaking for myself, I find that the feminine sensibility is a far more precise filter than any other to express what I have to say. In the realm of emotions, man is nearly always unable to feel reality as it exists. Having a tendency to dominate woman, he is tempted to hide some of her aspects from himself and see her as he wants her to be. There is nothing absolute in this area, but it seems to me that is at the heart of it."

One might call La Notte a proto-feminist movie, one which sees things through the eyes of the undervalued woman, not the vague and slightly complacent male. Mastroianni embodies Giovanni so much that one might easily forget his famous personal warmth, mistaking him for an ice cold intellectual incapable of real emotion. He is completely wrapped up in himself and his image as a writer, scorning money and wealth for integrity, which is all very good when it is his wife's inherited fortune he is living on. But the saddest part is that he realises his shortcomings at the end of the film, where he's gone wrong with his relationship and view on life, tragically when it's much too late. Again, it was a master class from Mastroianni, even if the film belongs to Moreau.

Ironically, given that it became one of his most acclaimed movies, and remains to this day a Mastroianni signature picture, he was never that keen on it. He had a few problems during its making. Firstly, he said, that he did not believe in his character's central crisis. Secondly, he did not enjoy working with Antonioni. "It was a very tense set," he recalled, adding that Antonioni did not like actors and that he and the screenwriter, Tonio Guerra, got into many disagreements. The one saving grace of the experience, he said, was his friendship with Moreau, the two being like two shipwrecked souls. It's funny to think that in the movie they are completely detached from one another, yet on the set relied on the other's support to get through.

Marcello accepted the part because the role of Giovanni reminded him of a writer friend he had, and he thought, rather optimistically, that he might be able to go into interesting areas with the part. But that evaporated away when he realised Antonioni's aim was much different to his own. Antonioni saw actors as a part of the whole picture, like colours in the painting, claiming once that he didn't like actors to become their own directors. Many actors had a hard time with him (Jack Nicholson was

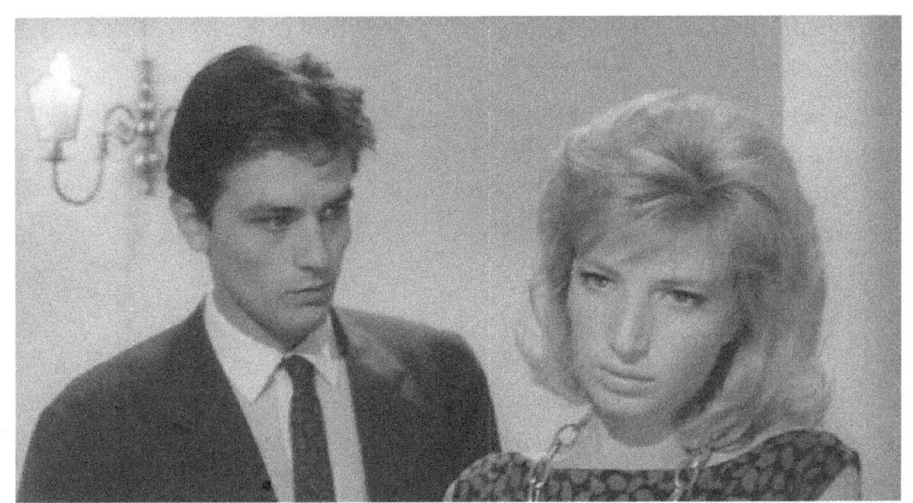

L'ECLISSE (1962)

rather proud to be the only actor to ever have gotten on well with him, when they made The Passenger over a decade after La Notte) and given that the easy going Mastroianni struggled with the director too says a lot. Though he may have had problems with the writer's struggle, a man in a fight between a life of integrity and one of wealth and privilege being offered on a plate by the millionaire tycoon, this is not present in the performance he gives. His every movement reeks of self importance, but an ego that is also fragile when all is said and done.

Michelangelo Antonioni continued in his pursuit for reflecting modern man's alienation, the intellectual concept of physical fulfilment juxtaposing with spiritual emptiness. One can take a still frame from any of Antonioni's films and they define alienation. Perhaps the most telling of his frames involve couples, a male and a female, who though together physically, or in close proximity at least, seem thousands of miles apart. There is an expectant gaze from the male, as if he's waiting for a reaction from the female, who in turn stares off camera, distracted by thoughts and dissatisfaction. In many ways it is the spaces between the people, whether in freeze frame or motion, that defines the films of Antonioni.

After his twin onslaught of L'Avventura (1960) and its follow up La Notte (1961), Michelangelo directed what is commonly regarded as the third part in this powerhouse trilogy, one many claim is actually the most ambitious of the three. Martin Scorsese himself later dubbed it the boldest of all.

Again, Antonioni uses a straight forward plot outline on which he hangs heavier, more eternal themes. It concerns Monica Vitti as Vittoria, who has just come out of an affair with Riccardo, a writer, and is now beginning a new one with Piero (Alain Delon), who works on the stock market. Vittoria herself works as a literary translator, a role in itself which could act as an absurd metaphor, she being a woman who deals in written communication but cannot get straight her relationships with those closest to her.

L'Eclisse might be seen by some as a straight forward love story, told through moody camerawork and equally moody performances. But this being Antonioni, there is so much more to the picture than its disconnected surface.

Every camera angle, every shot, every movement seems carefully and deliberately planned by Antonioni. Like La Notte, it moves at its own speed (i.e. barely at all) and dwells on buildings and backgrounds with delicacy. The architecture, as ever, is vital to L'Eclisse, and Rome, so booming with life and care free, if shallow, energy in la Dolce Vita, often here looks like an alien city observed from the eye of an outsider.

Once again, Monica Vitti is quietly, often silently compelling, Antonioni's perfect woman lost in a sea of meaninglessness. Whereas Jeanne Moreau had not enjoyed her previous experience with him, she had actually been an ideal Antonioni figure in La Notte, her slender frame starkly bold against run down city streets, her controlled, expressionless

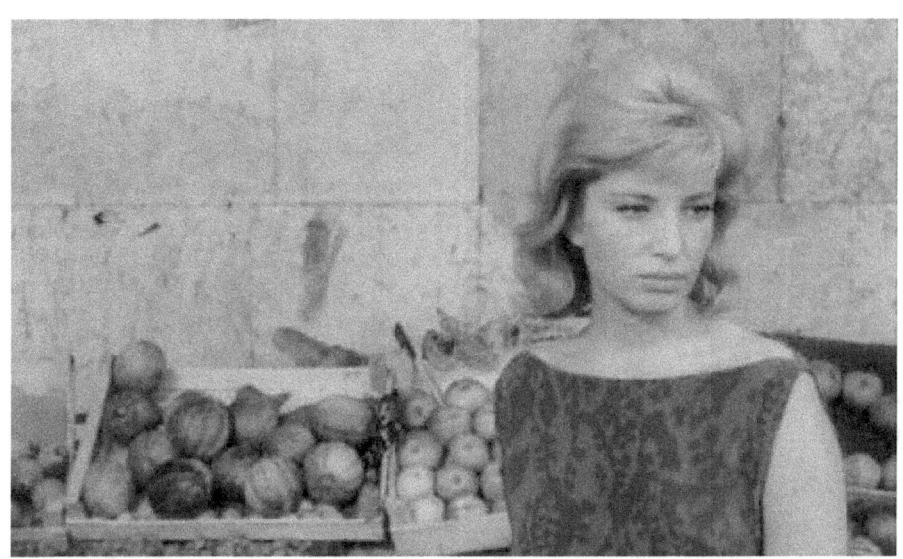

face contrasting harshly with the revelling so-called intellectuals at the all night shallow party. Vitti, striking in her own unique way, becomes so separated from her surroundings that it often feels like she's roaming around in another film all together.

L'Eclisse was another acclaimed outing for Antonioni, who was then on a roll as the premiere intellectual filmmaker. For all Fellini's psychological metaphors and living, waking dreams, Antonioni continued to be the master of understatement, leaving the internal as a great mystery, each human being an enigma to the other. Again, he won the Jury Prize at Cannes, earned a nod for the Palme d'Or and numerous other honours. To this day it is seen as a seminal film of its era, like L'Avventura, a major advancement for filmmaking.

In his documentary on Italian movies, Martin Scorsese speaks at length about L'Eclisse, saying it haunted him when he was a young man. Stating it was a distinct step forward in the art of storytelling, he also adds it "felt less like a story and more like a poem. The final seven minutes of L'Eclisse suggested to us that the possibilities in cinema were absolutely limitless."

Antonioni's reputation has taken something of a slow decline, especially outside Italy, in recent years. Whereas his contemporaries, especially Fellini, have seen their legacies become richer and more multi faceted, Antonioni is almost always seen as the singular priest of doom, the man who mourned communication and took great pains to remind us how separated we all were from one another. This gives the misguided impression that his films are depressing, which in my view they are not. They are certainly challenging, and may indeed be endurance tests for those used to a faster pace of movie. But anyone who has ever felt disconnected, disenfranchised and, most commonly of all, alienated even in the most superficially inclusive environment, Antonioni's works are endlessly relatable and consistently relatable.

L'Eclisse is among his finest works. An attack on the shallow, carelessness of a life lived in post-war bourgeois Rome, it is also Michelangelo's continued search for meaning, as seen through the eyes of the female.

"I especially love women," Michelangelo once said. "Perhaps because I understand them better? I was born amongst women, and raised in the midst of female cousins, aunts, relatives. I know women very well. Through the psychology of women, everything becomes more poignant. They express themselves better and more precisely. They are a filter that allows us to see more clearly and to distinguish things."

It is the fact he sees things from the feminine perspective, while highlighting the shallow emptiness of manhood and all its attached complications, that Antonioni remains a relevant filmmaker, one whose name, especially in this post-modern age, deserves to be uttered with more reverence more often.